Making Effective Presentations

MANCHESTER
O · P · E · N
LEARNING

KOGAN
PAGE

First published in 1992 as *Effective Presentation* by Manchester Open Learning, Lower Hardman Street, Manchester M3 3FP

This edition published in 1993 by Kogan Page Ltd

Kogan Page Limited
120 Pentonville Road
London N1 9JN

British Library Cataloguing in Publication Data

A CIP record for this book is available from the British Library.

ISBN 0 7494 1143 0

Printed and bound in Great Britain by Biddles Ltd, Guildford and Kings Lynn

Making
Effective

entations

INTRODUCING THE SERIES

Management Action Guides consist of a series of books written in an Open Learning style which are designed to be

■   user friendly

■   job related

Open Learning text is written in language which is easy to understand and avoids the use of jargon that is usually a feature of management studies. The text is interactive and is interspersed with Action Point questions to encourage the reader to apply the ideas from the text to their own particular situation at work. Space has been left after each Action Point question where responses can be written.

The Management Action Guides series will appeal to people who are already employed in a supervisory or managerial position and are looking to root their practical experience within more formal management studies.

Although the Management Action Guides are a series of books that cover all aspects of management education, each book is designed to be free standing and does not assume that the reader has worked through any other book in the series.

Titles in The Management Action Guides series are

Planning and Managing Change

Handling Conflict and Negotiation

People and Employee Relations

Achieving Goals Through Teamwork

Creating Customer Loyalty

Making Effective Presentations

Contents

GENERAL INTRODUCTION

How you conduct yourself when giving a presentation says as much about you, and your **attitude towards work** as it does about your grasp of the subject you're dealing with.

Any business greatly depends on its people's ability to **communicate and contribute effectively** both inside the company and externally to its customers and trading partners.

This ability to communicate and contribute effectively is essential

not only to	**but more importantly to**
■ inform	■ **enthuse**
■ illustrate	■ **persuade**
■ decide	■ **question**
■ discuss	■ **motivate**

Whether the contexts **you** get involved in are formal or informal, presentations should be seen as more than just a functional means of communication or decision making.

In this book, then, we shall consider

■ the importance of **creating the right climate** and adopting the **correct attitude** towards presentations

■ the **character and nature of your audience** and ways of adjusting your style of presentation appropriately

■ the need for **preparing in advance**

■ techniques for making more effective presentations by a thorough understanding of the different methods of **displaying statistical data and diagrams** and the most appropriate **audio-visual aids** to choose to display this information

■ a **professional** approach to **using** your audio-visual aids during your presentation

■ the importance of using language and techniques of public speaking in a controlled and planned way and the vital importance of **concise, clear expression**

1 PREPARING THE PRESENTATION

How you present yourself is as important as **what** you present - important not only to your own influence within your team, but also to the furtherance of the company's aim of uniting all of its workforce in a common mission.

You need, therefore, to identify **the many and varied contexts in which you will use your presentation**. Having established the context, you will need to understand **what attitude and approach to adopt** towards each context and each **type of audience** you may encounter.

You must also always bear in mind the more constant aim of promoting co-operation between sections in the company, displaying **high standards of professionalism** and responding to customer needs - both in terms of your function and in terms of the care and personal treatment you take.

Whenever you make a presentation, however informal it may be, you have to consider both the audience and your purpose. To create a successful presentation you must

- decide what you aim to achieve
- divide your overall aim into a list of achievable objectives
- know the kind of audience which is going to see and hear your finished work
- decide on your approach to get your aims accepted by the audience

This in effect means you have to tailor your aims to the audience.

1.1 YOUR AIM

First you have to decide on your overall objectives. What do you hope to have achieved at the end of your presentation?

It is essential that you define your objectives before you plan your presentation, or how else will you know that it was a success?

Ask yourself the following questions

- **Why** am I giving this presentation?
- Why have they asked **me**?
- What do I hope to **achieve**?
- How can I make it **interesting**?
- **How much** do the audience already know about the subject?
- Have they all the necessary **background knowledge**?

ACTION POINT 1

Think about a presentation that you have given recently. On reflection, do you think that the presentation was a success? If you had to give the presentation again, could you make any improvements?

Obviously, with hindsight you could have done a better presentation. But did you

- have your objectives firmly in mind?
- know the type of audience you were addressing?
- speak clearly using words that everyone understood?
- stimulate any appropriate action necessary?

A necessary part of the overall aim must be to get your message across. Whatever the context of your presentation and whoever constitutes the audience there are some fundamental principles for creating the right climate for the communication of information, the contribution of ideas and the furtherance of company values.

Setting the Scene

You must continually assess your audience for composition and mood, whilst remaining empathetic. This is a continuous process throughout a presentation, continually refining your response in the light of new evidence of their behaviour.

Professionalism

This means attending to facts, preparation and logistical arrangements. You must know your subject and be aware of the character of your audience. It means attending to detail while continually focusing on your purpose in speaking. It means using all speech and audio-visual media in the most effective way.

Tolerance

Accept the inexperience and ignorance of your audience and look upon it as a challenge rather than a problem. Assert your case or put over your point of view while tolerating the differing views of others.

Assertiveness

Apply any training you have had in this technique.

Assertiveness is based on the view that interpersonal human behaviour can be positioned on a continuous scale from the passive at one extreme to the aggressive at the other, with assertive behaviour in the middle ground.

Passive or submissive behaviour is usually not effective. Users of this type of behaviour seldom get what they want because they demonstrate a lack of respect for their own needs and rights. They allow others to deny them their rights and to ignore their needs.

At the other extreme there is aggressive behaviour. This behaviour is also not effective because the users express their feelings, needs and ideas at the expense of others.

Aggressive people invite resistance and hostility and they destroy goodwill, while passive people store up resentment and may then have explosive outbursts when they have 'earned the right'.

Use of assertive behaviour

■ utilises methods of communication which enable you to maintain your own self respect

■ defends your rights and personal 'space'

■ does not dominate members of an audience

Assertive behaviour uses these skills in listening and expressing yourself. Make sure that the aim **you** wish to achieve **is** achieved. Listen to comments made by your audience, but do not allow yourself to be sidetracked.

1.2 THE FRAMEWORK OF THE PRESENTATION

The key to a good and helpful structure in any written communication is to sort out your ideas and the relevant information before you put pen to paper. The most important point to understand here is that your presentation - no matter how informal - should have a **pre-determined structure.** That means

■ you should plan **in advance** the order of, and logical connection between the points you are going to put across

■ your presentation should be a series of **interconnecting** parts, each one capable of standing logically by itself

■ the interconnecting parts should link finally into the overall aim you wish to achieve

You should draw up two plans

■ the plan and structure of your **subject matter**

■ the plan and structure of **how you are going to present it**

These two plans will obviously be interconnected and interdependent and your plan ought to show the connections between the two. Do not be afraid of telling the audience about the pattern you are following.

Structure of Subject Matter

In general, your talk will be all the more effective if it has

■ a single consistent **theme**

■ **clear** objectives

■ **definable sections** which your audience can comprehend

Begin by gathering all your thoughts on the subject. You need to be as comprehensive and as wide-ranging as possible. You do not want to miss anything out, so have your own personal brainstorming session - or elicit the help of your colleagues. Next, you need to gather all this information into a clear, logical framework. You can do this by the traditional way of making lists etc, but there are other methods available.

Structuring Information

There are two techniques you can use to give structure to varied information

■ the brain pattern

■ outlining

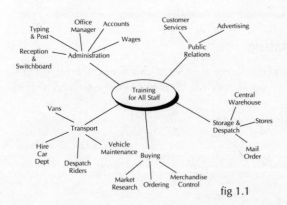

fig 1.1

Using **a brain pattern** helps when you have a number of random ideas and pieces of information to put into order and you do not need to restrict your thinking to straight lines. It was first developed by Tony Buzan in Use Your Head (BBC publications, 1984).

A brain pattern is a haphazard yet logical way of organising your thoughts.

It is constructed in the following way

1   Write the subject of your presentation in a box in the centre of a blank sheet of paper.

2   Draw branches leading from the box.

3   Write the main subjects you wish to cover on these branches.

4   Develop each section using sub-branches.

This may look at first glance like a very untidy and haphazard way of doing things, especially if you are someone who usually prepares by making lists.

The theory behind this approach is that the brain does not work as well in a linear format because the brain acts on 'triggers' which stimulate new thoughts. In effect, it thinks laterally rather than vertically. So although a completed brain pattern may appear untidy, to your brain it is clear and logical. It is a very effective way of marshalling your thoughts. It helps ensure that you don't miss out a major section. To bring everything together, draw different coloured lines around each section.

Using **an outlining system** encourages you to form your structure first and then fill in the details under each heading. First decide on the major divisions of your subject and then subdivide each of these major divisions into minor divisions. Then write about each subdivision separately from the others.

Much computer word processing software has outlining built into the program. The system allows you to concentrate on one aspect of your presentation at a time whilst giving the flexibility to jump from one area to another as the mood and inspiration takes you. The system is widely used (and taught) in the USA, but in the UK is sometimes held in suspicion as unduly restricting creative thought.

Structure of Presentation

Now you have a concise and comprehensive set of ideas for your presentation. Your next task is to prepare your framework for presentation which consists of

The **introduction** (beginning)	where you make contact with your audience
	introduce your subject and state the main theme
The **development** (middle)	where you explain the theme in more detail
	develop your theme and arguments
The **conclusion** (end)	where you summarise the main theme
	make recommendations (if necessary)

Some of the best business presentations, like some modern buildings, have their framework on the **outside** for everyone to see. You may want to give your audience advance notice of what is in store for them, particularly if what you have to say is complicated and lengthy.

There is every reason to keep your brain pattern or outline as your working document at this stage. It may become a mess of lines, arrows and boxes, or the divisions may not yet be in the right order but do not be tempted to head straight for the familiarity of lists and strings of sentences. Work out all the sections first. Only then redraft your brain pattern or outline in a tidier but no less detailed form.

Remember - a presentation which has been sold to you as 'just say a few words' may be promoted to your audience as the definitive, authoritative, final work on the subject. Probe beyond the face value of the task in hand and be prepared for the reality **as your audience sees it**.

ACTION POINT 2

Consider the sort of formal and informal presentations you may be required to make and try to categorise them. Are they primarily exercises in selling, informing, deciding, promoting or something else?

Are there any 'hidden' purposes or ulterior objectives involved? Have you ever been put in a situation where a presentation has been viewed by your audience differently from your own understanding of its purpose?

Write your comments below then continue reading the text.

Before the final structure is designed you must take account of the type and composition of your potential audience.

1.3 THE DIFFERENT AUDIENCES

Making a presentation is not an easy task, and some audiences will appear more daunting than others. But remember, you will be well prepared and it is likely you know more about the subject of your presentation than anyone else in the audience. The audience are probably hearing it for the first time and may have to assimilate new concepts.

There are two issues in considering audiences. One is their **mood and receptiveness**, and the other is their **social relationship** to yourself.

Mood and Receptiveness

There are two basic types of audiences - those who want to attend and those who have to attend. Within these basic categories there are variations and the categories can overlap. A work related audience can contain both types but consider someone who **has** to go to a presentation but who also **wants** to attend because they have a high motivation factor. You can judge beforehand what **basic** kind of category the audience will be composed of, but it is difficult to gauge beforehand how high the motivation will be.

Other external factors may affect motivation - how small or large the room is, how warm or cold it is, or even whether the sun is shining in the audience's eyes. These things you normally have to decide on the day of the presentation itself.

You can use management theories to categorise your audience. The hygiene factors are such things as the external environment and the pressure for attending the presentation. The motivators and dissatisfiers are the personal reasons for attendance and the existing level of knowledge of your subject that is already known by the audience.

The sure way to overcome problems is to make sure your preparation is as thorough as possible. In the worst case scenario your audience will listen but in a very negative manner. All the work will have to be done by yourself. You cannot afford to be ill-prepared. In the best case scenario your audience may be extremely participative and lead themselves on to the points you wish to make. Your preparation here will prevent any red herrings being followed.

It is vital that you use the first few minutes to take stock of your audience. Make the structure of your presentation use a variety of techniques in its early stages to test their receptiveness. Try slightly different approaches to see what kind of response you get. Ask for questions and comments at a reasonably early stage (when they have something to comment on). Then base the rest of the presentation on the feedback you get.

The Social Relationship

Now consider the different groups of people that you may be asked to speak to.

ACTION POINT 3

Make a list of all the different groups of people within your company who could make up your 'audience'.

Write your answers below and compare them with what follows.

Your list could have included

■   your superiors

■   your staff

■   managers from other sections

■   your peers

■   management trainees

ACTION POINT 4

In the introduction, we said you must enthuse, persuade, question and motivate your audience. Which of the above audience(s) would you particularly want to

(a)   enthuse?

(b)   persuade?

(c)   question?

(d)   motivate?

Jot down your ideas and then compare them with our ideas which follow.

The audience that you might like to **enthuse** could include superiors, your staff, managers from other sections, your peers and management trainees.

The audience you might like to **persuade** could include your superiors, managers from other sections and your peers.

The audience you might like to **question** could include your staff, your peers and management trainees.

The audience that you might like to **motivate** could include your staff, management trainees and your peers.

We will look at the categories of audience we used above.

(a)   Your Superiors

This can appear to be a very daunting audience - but think about what you have on your side

1   Your **expertise** - you already know more in depth about the subject at hand than they do or you would not have been asked to make the presentation.

2   Your **time** - you will have been given enough time both to prepare and to explain what you need to in your presentation **to the level which they require.**

3   Their **support** - they want you to do well. They may have had a say in your selection. They most certainly will want you to illustrate the company's high standards. They are on your side.

So do not be daunted or reticent, instead be

■   prepared

■   assertive

■   concise - they have no time to waste

■   accurate - you may be quoted

■   honest - if you do not know something and cannot reasonably be expected to know it then say so. **Do not bluff**

■   positive

Do not expect congratulations or even agreement at the end of your presentation. You should be treated courteously and in a businesslike way. The result of your presentation may only become apparent later.

(b)   Your Peers

This is probably the most difficult of all audiences. No matter how united the company is in its overall aims there will be rivalries between departments and conflicting short-term objectives. Your peers do not want you to lead them nor, unlike your superiors, do they have a stake in your success. In this context you must rely on professionalism and good preparation. Leave nothing to chance and never give the impression you are knowledgeable in an area where, in reality, you are unsure of your facts. Be positive when you are on safe ground without being aggressive or overly protective of your own department.

(c)   Your Staff

Here the subject matter of your presentation will influence your approach - for example, announcing the department's increased sales figures will require a lot less skill than departmental reorganisation! If you think your staff will behave as they normally do, or that there is little to learn about presenting some message to your collective group of people, then think again. The same people they may be - but as soon as they are collected together in one group and face you as a presenter they become an audience and behave like one. In practice this means they will expect a higher than normal standard of professionalism when it comes to

■   confidence, leadership and authority

■   preparation, knowledge and expertise

■   articulation, coherence and clarity

Your staff know you well - probably better than you realise. They appreciate your warmth and friendliness, but they won't tolerate weakness. You are their leader. They will also expect, and respond to, friendliness, equality of treatment, sincerity and your ability to judge their mood and temper. They want to be informed, entertained even, and certainly addressed as intelligent equals. But most of all they want to be **led**.

So again your talk should be

■   professional

■   enthusiastic

■   natural without being patronising

(d)   The Mixed Audience

Very often, of course, we don't have the benefit of an audience whose members are all of the same status, background, experience and knowledge. The problem with a mixed audience is that you may be unsure of **what** they already know, **what** they want to hear, **why** they are present and **how** they relate to one another. You will not know at what level to pitch your talk, what knowledge to assume, what kind of language to use and therefore from what angle to approach your subject.

In these instances you must be prepared to try and find out as much as you can about your audience before you start planning the content of your presentation. If you can arrange separate meetings for people of greatly differing expertise or interest, then do so. If you cannot, then always err towards the lower end of the scale of background knowledge so that everyone will **understand** what you have to say. The more knowledgeable members of the audience will have their knowledge confirmed. If you pitch your content towards the higher end of the scale, then less knowledgeable people would gain nothing but a sense of subconscious frustration from spending valuable time being talked at above their heads.

When speaking to a mixed audience remember to

■ let your audience **know** you have done your homework on them

■ let them know they are from different backgrounds and that, for some of them, some of what you may say will already be familiar. Get the audience on your side

■ use the opportunity to create a sense of common purpose. Let everyone in the audience believe that **they** need to hear what you are saying just as much as everyone else

■ keep things basic, explicit and clear

■ avoid jargon, in-words, private jokes (do not divide your audience into 'us' and 'them')

■ use natural pauses to remind various sections of your audience **why** they need to listen to what you are saying; talk from different angles

(e) The Hostile Audience

Occasionally you may be faced with a hostile audience. It could be, for example, disgruntled staff members because you are explaining new staffing levels; you may be asserting your group's interests in a context which unites other groups in opposition to you.

You have little on your side in these circumstances - so it is important that you use to the full the assets that you do have, which are

■ your **expertise** - this is your greatest asset, no-one will be as knowledgeable as you about the subject

■ **time** - the audience may be hostile because they have heard rumours that are completely unfounded. Use the time carefully so that you can not only put your case but also dispel their fears

Be sincere, open and honest with a tolerant and professional approach. Do not allow this approach to degenerate into weakness and on no account be apologetic either for your material or in your manner. Use the guidelines of assertiveness shown above.

Using Types of Audience

We have categorised the different types and composition of audience. This will influence the level of knowledge required and the kind of research you should conduct - for example, an in-depth subject knowledge or a broad, general awareness.

ACTION POINT 5

Imagine you are giving a presentation to the following audiences

(a)   Your staff - describing the new annual leave entitlements

(b)   Newly appointed marketing managers - describing new international services

(c)   A group of Company Directors - describing a new concept in executive travel

Answer the following questions about each presentation and type of audience

■   What are their educational and comprehension levels? What kind of language and ideas will they be able to understand readily?

■   Are you talking to people who are very familiar with the subject you are discussing (specialists)? Are you merely updating or expanding their knowledge?

■   Are you bringing to their attention something they were completely unaware of, or raising a subject that is entirely new to them?

■   Is your main aim to entertain, as well as to inform?

■   Are you giving a talk as part of a training or induction session?

■   What is your 'political' motive? To persuade someone to take action? To convince them of the wisdom of a particular course of action? To make sure they take account of particular factors in their decision-making and daily work?

■   How large will your audience be?

■   How light or serious should you be?

■   What vocabulary should you use?

■   How much background information is needed?

Write your answers and then continue with the text.

You should have borne the following points in mind

(a)   New annual leave entitlements should meet with a good reception, your staff will be eager to hear what you have to say. Make sure you understand all the details - perhaps the number of days entitlement has increased but a certain proportion must be taken during the winter months?

(b)   These are newly appointed marketing managers and may therefore have come from different departments, so make sure you use terms and phrases that everyone will understand. Invite questions but be wary of someone out to impress, rather than asking a justified question.

(c)   You are putting over your ideas about a new concept on executive travel so make sure you are precise, accurate and well-informed both on the new concept and existing travel arrangements for business executives.

1.4   PREPARATION AND PLANNING

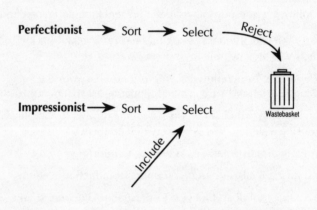

fig 1.2

Only now should you sort and categorise, select and reject all the material that you have collected for your presentation. Your approach to this process is very much dependent on your own style and particularly on your weaknesses. If you are by nature a perfectionist (and that is not striving after high quality, remember, it is striving at unattainable perfection in everything) then you should adopt a consciously ruthless approach to your sorting, selecting and especially rejecting. There is a tendency in perfectionists to put in everything they know or believe about a subject, irrespective of the specific angle from which they have been asked to approach it. You will very rarely be called upon to propound a 'world view' on a subject; what you say will never be the final word on the matter. Stick to the angle you have set yourself. Reject any 'padding'.

If on the other hand you are impressionistic and tend to skimp on detail - and you know that you do - work on the assumption that you are likely to omit the kind of information and background that will make your subject intelligible and accessible.

You should take an informed and honest view of your strengths and weaknesses in this process and constantly try to put yourself in your audience's shoes.

Remember, if you decide the purpose of a speech or presentation before you begin to work on it, your ultimate goal will be much clearer than if you approach your work with a less structured attitude.

Research your subject and be confident of what you say

There are a number of strategies you can adopt to bring your presentation to fruition.

Deciding the Approach

This will be different for each type of audience, but there are some rules which are applicable for all of them

1   Be **sincere and natural** - audiences will see through you straight away if you are not, so

    (a)   don't pretend to be who you are not

    (b)   speak from personal experience

2   Be **enthusiastic** - it makes your eyes sparkle - and enthusiasm is infectious!

3   Be **pleasant and friendly** - smile when you are introduced and at intervals throughout your speech. A smile, of course, does not have to be associated with humour - if you have a warm smile the audience will warm to you

4   **Use humour carefully** - some people are naturally witty, but most of us are not. Some people think they are being talked down to when it is used. But making your audience laugh with you is not as difficult as you might imagine because

    (a)   more often than not, they are listening to you with enthusiastic anticipation

    (b)   they have come to be entertained

Your aim is to express your ideas rather than impress your listeners. If in the course of making a clear statement, you also manage to create a good impression then that is a bonus. It is a bonus you are likely to win though, when you express yourself clearly.

Time

You must know for how long you will be expected to speak and for how long you will be allowed to speak. Unless you know these two pieces of information you will not be able to plan and rehearse what you have to say.

fig 1.3

Structure Your Commentary

Make sure you pace the presentation with a mix of formal and informal sections, with spoken and visual information, to retain the interest of the audience. People can only concentrate on one thing for about 10 minutes at a time, so shifting attention to a screen or a handout at judicious intervals is a must for full retention of concentration.

Help the audience follow the theme of your presentation easily. Don't be afraid to number the points you make, as in the following example

> 'In 1988 we saw three major trends in demand
>
> The first trend was . .
>
> The second trend . .
>
> The third trend . .'

This makes the individual points clearer and quicker to digest.

Statistical Information

Sources of your statistical data will depend very much on the topic you are tackling. In many cases they will be derived from departmental and section records, particularly when they are forming the theme of a presentation. In other instances you may need to draw upon

■ company records of finances, volume of business etc, which may be kept manually or generated in tabular or graphical form from computers

■ official statistics from government publications

■ industry-wide surveys and reports

We shall look more closely at presenting statistical information in Chapter 2.

You now need to build on your framework and put the contents into clear, concise English that your audience will understand.

Effective Opening Lines

The first few sentences that you say are crucial as they will influence the way your speech is received. You must know **exactly** what you are going to say in order to

■ create the right initial impression

■ capture the attention of **all** your audience

■ be interesting

ACTION POINT 6

Consider the following opening lines to a presentation entitled 'The Computer Communications Network within ABC Ltd'. Imagine you were a member of the audience and write down in the space on the next page what your reaction to each would be. Which do you think are good openers?

Note that judgement of these openers is very subjective and very much dependent on the composition of the audience, so perhaps you would like to start first by setting the scene. Compare your answers with our ideas in the text which follows.

1   'Today I'm going to give a presentation on the Computer Communications Network that has been set up within ABC....'

2   'How are the new computers going to bring increased efficiency between departments..?'

3   'Today I'm going to persuade you that introducing these new computers will save time...'

4   'The other day I was discussing the problems we are experiencing with the new computers with...'

5   'Computers are a waste of money..(pause)...unless we are going to train our staff to use them properly...'

6   ' A computer printed this letter in 10.6 seconds. If I had to send a letter to each departmental manager, the computer would save my department 4 hours work....'

7   'I must first apologise for the...'

Setting the scene	Comments
1	
2	
3	
4	
5	
6	
7	

Our ideas on each introduction are as follows

1   A boring introduction - after all, you know the title already or you wouldn't be in the audience.

2   A good opening line. The audience will instinctively think of reasons why the computers will bring increased efficiency. As you give your reasons, your audience will warm to you as you say the ones they thought of.

3   This is likely to provoke a hostile response, such as 'Oh no you're not!', 'We're OK as we are', 'We like doing it this way'.

4   An informal approach. You admit that there are problems which will get the audience on your side, so you will have their attention as they will be listening for ways to resolve the problems.

5   A good opening that will shock the audience - the speaker has now got their full attention.

6   Numbers and statistics at the beginning of a presentation can put your audience off, it is much better to introduce and illustrate them in the middle of your speech.

7   Your audience may doubt your ability and will certainly feel it's going to be an unprofessional presentation.

Language and Style

You do not gain any respect for trying to be someone you are not. So the first and most important point is always feel comfortable with the words you use. You can adjust your style and your language quite considerably to match the occasion and the people you are talking to and yet still feel comfortable yourself. The aim should be to express yourself clearly in language which is pitched at the lowest common denominator of expectation and understanding of your audience.

So what do you actually say (or avoid saying) to achieve this clear communication and understanding? It is easier to use the right words when talking to someone you know well. When you have worked alongside someone for a while, you probably assume that you have a reasonable understanding of each other's level of knowledge and experience. Even so, there are some things to take care to do or not do in order to be sure of a clear communication.

The Words you Choose

You can tell that someone has a real mastery of their subject when they communicate in everyday language without being patronising. This means using clear and concise words, sentences and paragraphs. Here are some examples for you to use.

Sentences For Formal Occasions

How you use sentences depends on the formality of the occasion.

Compare the two sentences below

1   Amongst friends or colleagues

> 'Got a job as a holiday rep during the summer vac - spoke the local lingo too!'

2   At an interview

> 'I studied tourism and modern languages at Bath University. During the summer holidays I was employed by a tour company as a holiday representative in Spain'

Amongst friends and family, you will probably speak in a kind of familiar shorthand. When you are in a formal or semi-formal situation, you need to construct your sentences more carefully, as in the second example. It is a sign of respect for your listeners that you opt for a clear sentence structure, avoiding the more relaxed style linking in short phrases.

There is always a danger when using a more formal sentence construction of using words that are longer and less easy to understand. Guard against this. Be yourself and use words that you are comfortable with.

Use Technical Terms with Caution

If you are giving your presentation to an audience whose technical background you are uncertain of, check it out. Beware of incorrect terminology and be as exact as your subject permits. If there are non-specialists, don't neglect them. Give non-technical summaries of the main points of your argument.

Avoid Jargon, Acronyms and Tautologies

Avoid jargon, buzz words and in-words because

53996

- not everyone will know what you are talking about

- words can lose their precise meaning because of over use or use in different contexts - for example, 'hot' can mean

    (i)   electrically live to an electrician

    (ii)   at a high temperature to the majority of people

    (iii)   potential profit to a receiver of stolen goods

- language purists can get annoyed at the way fashionable words are misused, eg. brilliant

Don't use acronyms or abbreviations which only your department fully understands.

Do not say the same thing twice over using different words, for example

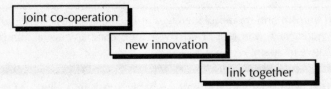

joint co-operation

new innovation

link together

This does not mean that you should start revising your grammar and reading the dictionary - on the contrary, use words which you feel comfortable with without being too figurative.

ACTION POINT 7

Think of some words that could be called your jargon, ie. words that are over-used, misused or peculiar to you and your department. Divide them up into two groups

1   Your **personal** jargon, ie. the words that you personally could use less or avoid in future.

For example

'The players were tremendous, but I was **sick as a parrot** when we let that goal in.'

2   Your departmental jargon, ie. the words that are used, abused, over-used or misused by you, your colleagues and your staff.

Jot down your answers and then continue with the text.

Your answers will be personal but it is important to realise that while **you** may feel comfortable using such phrases, some of them may be hackneyed or incomprehensible to others, especially those outside your department.

Be Clear and Precise

Be precise, find an exact word or phrase, not a vague, messy long-winded alternative (Again this is vital when explaining numbers).

don't say	say
gives an indication of	shows
has some impact upon	affects
should not be taken as meaning	does not mean
increasing over time	rising

Clear thinking about your subject will lead to clear speech and clear writing. Be satisfied with nothing less.

Linguistically, there is a modern trend away from simple descriptive terms towards 'advertising agency' language - that is, abstract words and high flown terminology which are difficult to relate to experience and almost impossible to imagine, for instance

'The speaking element of this volume is front-loaded'

which means

'The notes on speaking are at the beginning of the book'

Don't be tempted to use this type of language. Words are there to make your meaning crystal clear, not to cloud it.

ACTION POINT 8

Read the following paragraph. If you heard this speech, what would be your immediate thoughts?

'We must set our sights high and make the best possible use of our resources, both human and material. We must show our competitors that we continue to be a force to be reckoned with and ensure that at the end of the next financial year we are once again in an unassailable position.'

Jot down your answer and then continue with the text.

The problem with this speech is that it actually says very little in concrete terms. It is all well and good to threaten improvement, but the audience needs to know what needs to be done in a practical sense.

A better way to put it would be as follows

'We are determined to stay ahead of our competitors next year. A 10% increase will keep us on top. We must work together to achieve that. It will not be easy - but we can do it. If the inspectors never had to reject a unit as a second we would be well on the way. Seconds are nearly right, but not quite. If we got them absolutely right we would increase output by 5%. That's half of the increase we need.'

Now the speaker has not only set the target but has also described one way of helping to meet the target. We can imagine what is needed and have at least one idea of how to achieve it.

Avoid Long Sentences

Avoid long sentences, especially those with lots of qualifying clauses and/or figures as they will only confuse your audience.

ACTION POINT 9

Read the following sentence

'In the region of 60% of all visitors use air and 40% sea transport to reach Britain, and since UK airlines and shipping carry a large part of this traffic, overseas visitors' fare payments to UK carriers of some £850 million in 1982 rose to more than £1,000 million in 1983, and to £1,100 million in 1984.'

Rewrite the sentence just quoted in short, crisp sentences that would be appropriate in a personal presentation.

Check your version with that suggested below.

The extent to which you have broken the sentence down will be based partly on your personal style and partly on the type of audience you have identified. In its simplest form you may have written

'Around 60% of all visitors use air transport to reach Britain and the other 40% use sea transport. UK airlines and shipping carry a large part of this traffic. Overseas visitors' fare payments to UK carriers were about £850 million in 1982. They rose to more than £1,000 million in 1983, and in 1984 they reached £1,100 million.'

Be Sensitive to Your Audience

If the audience is hostile or prejudiced, make sure your commentary is soundly structured and your own attitude is positive. If you know what the counter arguments are, refute them in what you say. But don't raise criticisms yourself - there is no reason why you should sow the seeds of scepticism.

For example, don't say

'You may think this is a disappointing percentage because..'

Do not confirm their suspicions as in

'It is true that the number has dropped although we denied this before..'

Be thorough and professional at all times.

Make Facts and Figures Relate

A string of facts and figures is unlikely to be successful in catching a listener's imagination. Try to make a simple, easily understood link between factual details and everyday experience as in the following example

'Overheads in this department have gone up 7.9 per cent in the last year from £86,476 to £93,307. This means that each unit we turn out now costs 4 pence more to produce.'

Try to imagine for yourself what the practical implications of your words are for your listener.

We have now covered the content, language and format that you will use in your presentations. Your next task is to put all this information together.

1.5 WRITTEN SCRIPTS AND NOTES

Few people can give a presentation of more than a few minutes without some form of notes. You should prepare notes that **you** feel happy with. If you are unsure how detailed to be, then always err on the side of completeness. If the words flow on the day - all well and good - but if they don't, you always have something to fall back on. **Never** leave statistics or quotations to the unreliable mercy of your memory.

Do **not** read verbatim from a script unless your presentation is entirely technical and detailed - it will prevent you from using posture and eye contact to your benefit. It also results in a boring and uninspiring presentation.

As a general rule you should at this stage write your presentation out **in full** - it will make you think more deeply and logically about each section. Prepare notes and memory aids from this draft. If your presentation is formal and a text is going to be made available to your audience make sure that your final memory aids do not deviate from the full text of your speech.

fig 1.4

Design your notes in a way that will make them a real **aid** not just a security symbol.

Use a form and size of writing or type that is clear, large and vivid. Use different colours for quotes, statistics and visual aid cues. Do whatever you can to stop your notes degenerating into a mass of blue ink. Postcard-sized cards are extremely useful for your notes, they can be shuffled, they fit into your pockets, they do not tear easily, you have less to rewrite if you make a mistake in drafting and they do not flap about in nervous hands.

Remember

- use different colours
- number your cards
- write quotations, statistics and sources in full
- include visual aid cues for slides, transparencies etc
- use highlights for emphasis
- use diagrams or drawings to remind **you** what happens next

1.6 REHEARSING

Rehearsing your presentation serves many purposes - but only when it is done thoroughly. You should try to re-create as many of the likely circumstances of your presentation as you can, particularly in formal contexts.

Check for

- **timing** - the length of each section and the full presentation at the appropriate speed

- **duplications** and **omissions**

- **sense** - many words and phrases make perfect sense until you actually hear yourself utter them

- **visual aid cues**

- **pronunciation** - do some words or phrases look fine when written but sound odd, confusing or dissonant when spoken?

We will look at the spoken delivery of your presentations in more detail later in the unit, for now you should simply be aware of the necessity of knowing in advance what it will **sound** like on the day.

CHAPTER SUMMARY

Having completed this chapter you should now

- realise the importance of promoting the right climate of professionalism and tolerance in your presentations

- understand the importance of a correct planning procedure

- understand the attitude and approach to adopt for each type of audience you may encounter

- appreciate the need to use a clear, precise approach to ensure greater comprehension from the listener

If you are unsure of any of these areas, look back and re-read the relevant part(s) of the text.

2 PRESENTING VISUAL INFORMATION

In this chapter, we shall look at ways of emphasising and illustrating your presentation with visual information such as charts, graphs and diagrams, paying particular attention to statistical data. For many people the word 'statistics' conjures up a daunting prospect of facts and figures which are difficult to define or understand. Yet we all use statistics both in our personal and working lives and the increasing use of computer systems brings us an ever-increasing amount of numerical data.

As part of your presentation, you will almost certainly need to convey some form of data to your audience. You will need to present this information in a clear, concise form so that it will be easily understood. Tabular presentation is probably the most accurate way, with lists of figures accurate to perhaps several decimal places. However, your aim is to **demonstrate what the lists of figures show** in a form that is clear, accurate, uncomplicated and easily understandable to **all** your audience. To do this you will need to use some form of **pictorial representation** that can be displayed in such a way as to allow all your audience to see and digest the information at the same time.

Pictorial representation is a much more interesting way of presenting data than lists of facts and figures - each new chart will renew your audience's attention and bring added interest to your presentation.

We begin this chapter by looking at ways of **selecting** and **analysing** statistical data. We shall consider the main types of pictorial representation such as **charts and graphs,** as ways of displaying this data to best effect so that the key features you wish to present can be easily recognised.

2.1 STATISTICAL DATA

Whichever way you choose to present your statistical data, give your audience sufficient time to digest them, take notes, refer to handouts or do whatever is necessary.

Do not understate statistics or rush past them, particularly if they are central to your theme. If statistics are worth mentioning then they are worth emphasising. Use pauses, repetition and well-timed visual aids to make the statistics **stand out**.

Put statistics in their true perspective: explain their meaning, their source, their reliability, their significance and, unless it is already clear, whether they are good, bad or indifferent. This, obviously, is particularly important when your audience is made up of people who are not familiar with your department's work.

We come across statistical information every day of our lives, for instance

- data on the day-to-day working of your section
- comparative costs for a piece of new equipment for the department
- even the number of hours of sunshine in various towns and cities shown in the newspaper

It is easy to see that there is great diversity of types of statistical information, but what do they all have in common?

Words and Statistics

Perhaps you noticed that they all involve the use of numbers - that is they include quantification - an expression of a particular or definite amount of something.

Consider the following briefing on advertising expenditure.

A Marketing Manager displays a table on an overhead projector and says to the audience

> 'This is a table showing details of advertising expenditure and sales revenue for the last five years'

Consider in contrast

> 'We were very pleased with last June's TV campaign: as you can see, ticket sales rose by 4% during June and July and our share of the domestic market increased by 2%. That's why we would like to extend the TV campaign into July this year'

Here the Marketing Manager has made a direct input by analysing, explaining and drawing conclusions from the statistical data, making a more interesting, thought provoking presentation for the audience.

When presenting statistical information you must always give your audience all the pieces of the jigsaw and show them unambiguously how these fit together.

We need words to qualify or fully explain the numerical statement

This rule applies to all your statistical data, whatever form of presentation you choose.

Selecting Statistical Data

The data you have collected may be in many different forms

■ scribbled down from a meeting

■ tabulated in a computer printout

■ taken from an official or business report or press release

Whatever its original format you must now decide how to reorganise it so that it complements the theme of your presentation. **Select** the numbers that are really necessary to give your message 'bite'. Obviously, you should not use this selection process to eliminate embarrassing or inconvenient figures but you do not want to give such exhaustive detail that your audience becomes bogged down and your points are lost.

Ask yourself questions like

■ how will these figures advance my narrative or argument?

■ how will they aid understanding of the subject?

Be Informative

Every chart and graph you include should be relevant to the trend of your argument or explanation, and should add something new, have an impact, and highlight the points you are making in the most effective way possible.

It will help if the audience has something to compare or relate the new statistics to - such as last year's figures, a rival company's performance, seating capacity and staffing levels of other aircraft - anything that will help them get the picture in focus and perspective.

ACTION POINT 10

How do you think that irrelevant statistics could weaken the impact of your presentation?

Compare your ideas with what follows.

Irrelevance has several destructive effects

- ■ if it stems from repetitiveness ie. making the same point again for the sake of it, it is boring
- ■ if it is the result of seeking to impress, it will distract or confuse
- ■ it is always irritating and time-wasting

Don't fall into the trap of including statistics because you think they will impress, or labour a point that you have already made elegantly and forcefully.

When planning what statistics to include in your presentation, keep the central theme of what you will say firmly in mind.

Be Human

Statistics can seem impersonal, dehumanising and alienating -

'One death is a tragedy whereas twenty thousand is a statistic'

When you are communicating numbers, these numbers will often relate to **real people in real situations**. You know that people are the greatest resource of your organisation, and that they need to be thought of and cared for as individuals; you must therefore guard against the tendency to slip into

- sweeping generalisations and stereotyping

- portraying people as statistical 'problems'

- thinking about people in quantitative rather than qualitative terms

Be aware of these dangers when choosing your words, both in commentary and as headings on charts and tables.

Be Consistent

Use the same words and figures as appear in the chart or table. If you have categorised 'female clients' on your visuals, don't define them as 'women customers' in your commentary. Don't refer to numbers in your presentation and then transfer these into percentages on your charts. Your audience will be relating what you say directly to what they see, so don't confuse them by giving a verbal message that differs from the visual one. Repeating your words will reinforce your message, not detract from it.

Be Professional and Keep Your Perspective

Statistics are only tools, aids and indicators. They can only describe, compare and predict. They are never a replacement for values nor a justification for poor customer care, nor can they dictate the correct course of action. Do not use words to suggest they can do so. Avoid emotive and derisive language such as

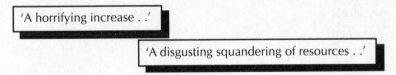

'A horrifying increase . .'

'A disgusting squandering of resources . .'

Don't misinform your audience. You could do this unintentionally unless you

- make sure that what you are saying will be comprehensible to your audience

- make sure that they understand the exact meaning of what you are talking about

Don't abuse statistics to

- make unwarranted demands on resources

- attack other sections or otherwise undermine trust and support

- imply criticisms of the organisation, or parts of the organisation, to outside audiences

Let's look at some different ways of illustrating your statistical information.

ACTION POINT 11

What different ways of illustrating and presenting statistical data can you think of?
Try to think of as many as you can and write your list below, then compare it with
what follows.

Your list could have included

■ bar charts

■ histograms

■ graphs

■ pie charts

■ pictograms

■ maps

■ break-even charts

In this chapter we shall look at the most frequently used charts and graphs. In
the appendix we have covered the less commonly used ones. The subject
matter of your presentation will determine both the number and types of charts
etc that will be most appropriate for you.

For instance, if you are doing a statistical presentation such as 'The Anatomy
of the Workforce within ABC Ltd', then the appendix charts and graphs will be
much more relevant than if the subject of your presentation is , for example,
'The Introduction of a New Advertising Campaign'.

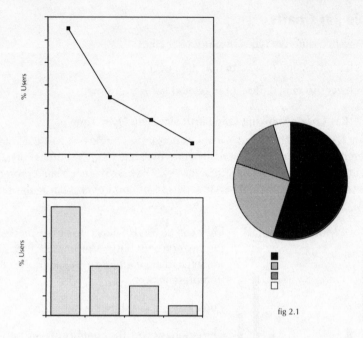

fig 2.1

2.2   BAR CHARTS

Bar charts are probably the most common form of diagram for presenting and comparing data.

There are a number of different types of bar chart

- simple bar charts
- grouped bar charts
- component bar charts
- percentage component bar charts
- back to back bar charts
- floating bar charts
- deviation bar charts

We shall look at simple bar charts here in the text, the others (as we noted above) are explained in the appendix.

Simple Bar Charts

There are two different types of simple bar chart

■　charts showing one particular item over time

■　charts showing different but related items over time

(a)　Bar Charts Showing One Particular Item Over Time

The simplest form of bar chart is a row of bars representing one particular item at different times eg. monthly rainfall figures over one year, the number of daily flights from one airport over a particular week. The height of each bar represents the amount of that particular service, person or good over a particular time period.

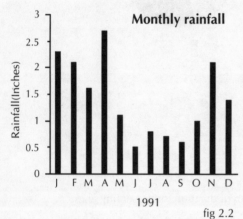

fig 2.2

They can be used to illustrate simple pieces of information only, but give an immediate visual impact and are therefore very suitable for use in a presentation.

Look at this chart showing rainfall.

The emphasis is on the **quantity** of rain that fell in **each month**. Your audience will notice immediately the **highest and lowest levels** of monthly rainfall - that is, which were the wettest and which the driest months. This would not be as obvious in a list of figures.

(b)　Bar Charts Showing Different but Related Items Over Time

A similar application is a row of bars representing quantities of different, but related items during the same time period. In this case you should arrange the bars by size, starting with either the highest or the lowest. The data will be much clearer and therefore assimilated faster. Although each bar corresponds to a different item, all can still be shaded or coloured identically.

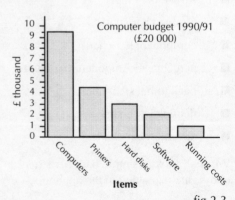

fig 2.3

ACTION POINT 12

Look at the bar chart in figure 2.3 above showing a computer budget for 1990/91.

What information is immediately conveyed from looking at the chart?

Write your answer in the space provided and then compare it with the following text.

Guidelines for Drawing Bar Charts

You want your charts to look professional, so follow these guidelines

■ choose convenient dimensions for the axes. If you wish to highlight the differences between figures which are large, you may wish to put a clear break in the scale

■ make all the bars the same width

■ make the width of each bar about one-fifth of the length of the longest bar

■ leave a half-bar width between bars and at each end

■ give a general heading to each diagram and label the scale and bars clearly

■ make sure the bars are in proportion for the relative sizes of the quantities they represent

■ bar charts can be shown either vertically or horizontally. With the horizontal format, you can label the horizontal bars directly and easily without having to use abbreviations. It is best to label at the left. With vertical bars labelling is difficult as space is limited - you may have to include a key

■ don't write the label inside the bar itself

■ don't draw three-dimensional bar charts - they only complicate the visual image

Cost of Replacement Equipment per Employee 1989-91

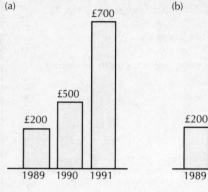

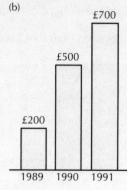

fig 2.4

Look at these charts.

In chart (a) the elements are wrongly proportioned and give a misleading impression.

Chart (b) shows the correct proportions.

The **quantity** on the Y axis of a bar chart **does not have to be numbers**. It can, for example, be such things as

- percentages
- rates per thousand of the potential population

2.3 LINE CHARTS (GRAPHS)

Line charts enable us to display data and identify trends which occur over periods of time. They are well-suited for highlighting **changes** in quantities over such time periods and are widely used in the press and on television, in text books and reports.

There are a several different types of line graphs

- single line graphs
- multiple line graphs
- scatter diagrams
- band charts

We shall look at single line and multiple line graphs in this chapter, the others are in the appendix.

The Single Line Chart

In the chart over the page, the X axis represents time, measured in years, and the Y axis measures company profits, measured in thousands of pounds.

The plot points for given years are connected up showing increases and decreases in the amount of profit each year. The plot points are clearly marked in this instance to show how the line itself was developed.

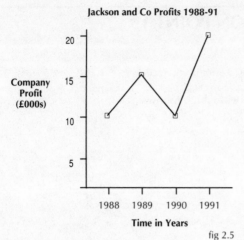

fig 2.5

The line graph has the following main elements

■   the line from which the form gets its name

■   the axes on which the scale of the chart is measured

They are relatively easy to understand and make a good visual impact.

The Multiple Line Chart

Multiple line charts help your audience **compare trends** in separate but related variables. This type of chart can be useful in presenting such things as estimates and costs of a project.

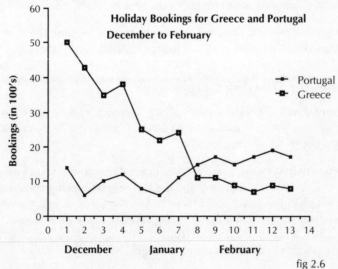

fig 2.6

ACTION POINT 13

Look at the graph above.

What pieces of information do you notice immediately?

Check your ideas with ours in the text which follows.

You should have noticed that

■ although the bookings of holidays to Greece started off higher than for Portugal in December, by Week 8 they had fallen below those to Portugal and remained there for the rest of the period shown

■ the number of holidays booked for Greece has varied during the period to a much greater degree than bookings for Portugal. Whereas bookings for Greece fell quite steeply in the period, those for Portugal varied much less, rising fairly steadily from the sixth week, until the last week of February when bookings for both countries fell

This clearly illustrates that the graph is more useful for 'making sense' of the statistics than detailed tables or lists of figures in these circumstances.

Guidelines for Drawing Graphs

The horizontal axis (X axis) usually shows changes in time. It is always measured in units that form **a continuous series**, whether it is being measured in milliseconds, minutes, days, years etc.

It is important to make sure that, whatever interval of distance you choose to represent one unit of measurement, you **use this regular spacing consistently** along the length of the axis. Even if there is, for example, one year for which there is no data, you must still leave the appropriate space for that year. You cannot just miss it out. If you do, you will affect the slope of the graph, so that it is not comparable at all points along its length.

The vertical axis (Y axis) denotes the **quantity** of the particular objects, people or service whose change is being charted. The further apart the units of measurement on this scale ie. the larger the scale - the steeper will be the resultant graph lines.

The intersection of quantities and times are plotted on the chart at the appropriate points. With a line graph you will always put your message over more effectively if you

■ use some form of pointer or highlighting to indicate the factors causing a sharp upturn, a downturn or a plateau

■ use appropriate magnitudes on your axes to illustrate movements in the chart fully. Make sure they will be clearly noticeable to your audience

■ explain any unusual factors that cause unexpected movement

2.4 PIE CHARTS

The pie chart, or divided circle chart, is a visually appealing way of showing percentage components of a given total. The segments represent the proportions of the whole for each individual variable. Have a look at the pie chart showing airline staff by occupational group, given as a percentage of the total aircrew.

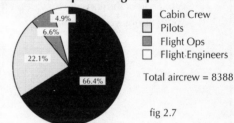

Aircrew occupational groups

■ Cabin Crew
□ Pilots
▨ Flight Ops
□ Flight·Engineers

Total aircrew = 8388

fig 2.7

You can see immediately that it shows the broad relative proportions of how any total is divided up.

The segments must be measured accurately to correspond in size with the percentage of the total they form. You have already come across this requirement in bar charts, where each of the bars must be the correct height in relation to the others.

You can work out the exact number of degrees of the total circle each segment should take and using a protractor measure each segment accurately. We calculate the number of degrees in the circle which each segment should fill by taking the percentage which that segment represents of the whole total and multiplying it by 360 (the number of degrees in the circle).

For example, a 5 per cent segment should occupy 5/100 of the circle. Multiplying 5/100 by 360 we find that 18 degrees of the circle would represent that percentage of the whole.

Your pie chart should include

- the percentage of each segment
- the total number of the whole it represents
- sensible shading to differentiate the slices
- a key

The segments are usually drawn in a clockwise direction, starting from '12 o'clock'. Begin with the factor to which you wish to draw most attention. This need not be the largest factor, it may just be more relevant to the theme of your presentation. If there is no specially significant factor, order your segments logically - eg. from largest to smallest - to make the figure as easy to interpret as possible.

ACTION POINT 14

See if you can recall any pie charts you have seen recently in newspapers, on television or in other people's presentations.

What sort of things were they depicting? Make a list, and add to it any other suitable applications you can think of.

You will probably have thought of such things as the following

- staffing divided by kinds of work done
- market shares of companies at a given point in time
- political parties' representation in parliament
- budgetary breakdowns
- income and expenditure figures

Before you decide to use a pie chart you must be sure of two things

■   that you can represent all of your figures in a way that will create visible, sizeable segments of the pie

■   that the pie represents a real, meaningful whole

The number of segments it's reasonable to put into a pie depends on how it will be presented. In a presentation, you cannot with safety include as many as you would in a chart that forms part of a report or other written submission.

Multiple Pie Charts

A pair of pie charts can be used to compare the same kinds of things as single pie charts, but

■   at different points in time, eg. 1979 and 1989

■   for different groups, eg. one showing a breakdown for males, another for females

■   for different criteria , eg. the way money is earned and the way it is spent

There are drawbacks to presenting a series of pie charts simultaneously, particularly when different groups of criteria are described.

Multiple pie charts are a rather crude method of comparing data, and can only give a clear idea of dramatic changes in the share of one component, or show that one or more factors have been eradicated and replaced by something else.

Where the size of the 'whole' represented has changed over time, the direction of change can be indicated, in broad terms, by changing the size of the circle.

Non-Statistical Information

Your presentation may contain no statistical information, but you should still consider visual illustrations.

ACTION POINT 15

Why do you think visual communication is important in a presentation?

Write down your answers in the space provided and then compare them with ours.

Visual representation will enhance your presentation in several ways

- it reinforces your commentary

- it keeps the audience's attention by providing variety

- it makes the words easier to understand, particularly for an audience with differing abilities, who may not all be able to digest spoken communication at the same rate

- it reduces the number of words necessary

Flow Diagrams

These diagrams are useful for showing the key steps in a process. Have a look at the flow chart on staff appraisal. This shows the sequence of steps taken to see whether an employee can perform a particular task.

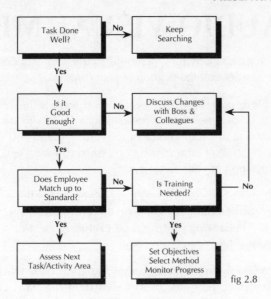

fig 2.8

CHAPTER SUMMARY

Having completed this chapter you should now

■   be familiar with basic chart types and the kind of data relationships each will highlight

■   know how to design charts, avoiding confusion and over complexity

■   understand the basic principles relating to scales and units of measurement, clarity and compatibility, which will be applicable in a wide range of statistical contexts

■   be aware of the importance of planning and preparation - and the counter effects that result from an unprofessional approach

If you are uncertain about any of these areas, look back and re-read the relevant part(s) of the text.

3 AUDIO-VISUAL MEDIA

Your aim in making any presentation is to use fully and competently all the different means of communication at your disposal.

Some people respond best to the spoken word, some to the written word, others to pictorial or diagrammatic representations, others to flow charts, circuit diagrams and so on. Your choice of the various audio and visual media will depend on the type of information or message you want to communicate and the predisposition of your audience.

Used well, audio and visual media can not only add to the impact of what you say but can also communicate concepts that are difficult to put into words. They are a means of **enhancing** your message, **capturing** attention and **increasing** the scope of your subject matter.

And yet, probably more presentations are spoiled by the inappropriate or incompetent and careless use of audio -visual media than by any other cause. You will need therefore to **choose the right medium or media** for your presentation. In order to gain the best advantage from these media, you will need to **prepare, plan and test your audio and visual aids** before you make your presentation. This will include the need to **practise the skills required to use equipment properly**.

3.1 YOUR OPTIONS

There are several ways of presenting data using different audio and visual media. Before you decide which methods to choose, think about why you are wanting to illustrate your speech and what you hope to achieve. In particular

- do not be tied down by custom, habit or the 'done thing'

- do not assume you **must** use audio and visual media because it is 'expected' - your message may be best put across by straight talking, in which case images and extraneous sounds will only distract your audience and detract from your words

- be imaginative - where images or sounds will assist you, think first about your various options. Try to assess the value of as many ideas as possible before you make your choice

- if you **mix** your media try to match the various formats you use - maintain a theme running through and across your presentation methods: the same terminology, logos, quantities, colours

■ above all first think 'Why?' Ask yourself what you hope to achieve beyond giving your audience something to pay attention to other than yourself

These are the factors you must take into account when you **start** to plan your presentation. In general the best way of illustrating your talk will be dictated by the general approach you select for your presentation. This will depend on

■ the amount and complexity of the information to display

■ the size and composition of your audience

■ the facilities available in the venue

ACTION POINT 16

Make a list of the audio and visual media you might decide to use in your presentations.

Write your list below and then compare your answers with ours which follow.

Your list could have included the following

chalkboard	whiteboard
flipchart	overhead projector
slide projector	tape recorder
cine film	tape-slide projector
models and charts	video cassette recorder
real objects	written and pictorial handouts

We will now take a detailed look at all the audio-visual media that may be available to you.

Chalkboards and Whiteboards

These are still the most popular for many people but are quite primitive by comparison with other available options. Their biggest drawback is that you cannot prepare much beforehand because you will lose the element of surprise. They are ideal for

■ building up a case

■ collecting ideas

■ brainstorming

■ collecting questions from the audience

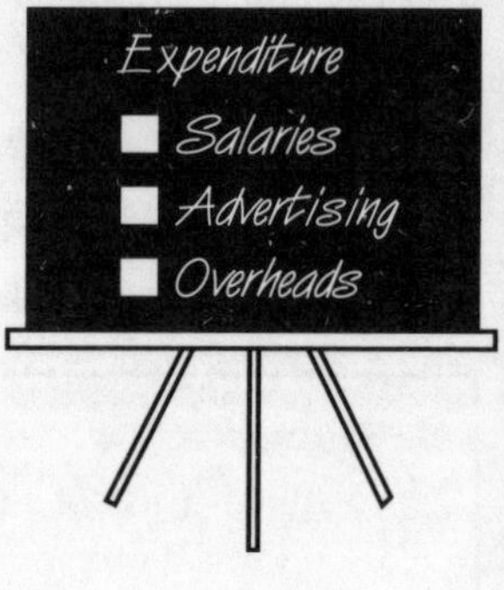

In fact the chalkboard and whiteboard are excellent for any task that requires a quick but temporary collection of words or images as an aid to memory.

Do not use either board for tasks which require

fig 3.1

■ permanence

■ style

■ impressiveness

■ the projection of an image

They should be used only as large, convenient jotters and short term memory aids. To put it bluntly - writing something like 'ABC Ltd aims at excellence' on a chalkboard simply undermines the message.

These boards have their disadvantages

■ once the board is full and you want to move on, you can't store the information

■ it is hard to get them completely clean

■ it is hard to control your writing

■ chalkboards are dusty

■ the writing on whiteboards is sometimes too thin for those at the back to see

■ your pens may dry out and you may develop the unfortunate mannerism of trying to shake the ink down

Flipcharts

A flipchart is a large block of paper that rests on an easel. The sheets are turned over as they are finished with and the next clean sheet or prepared diagram is then ready for use. They come into their own when feedback and interaction are needed. They are invaluable training aids. However, don't use them when you need to impress your audience for high profile publicity or for public relations as they don't project an image of excellence.

Be sure that each flipchart is

- **easily understood** - headings and labels must be clear. If the chart is to be on display as a background reference, explain its importance at an early stage

- **easily read** - use dark, thick pens and crayons. No one can read yellow print on shiny paper that's reflecting the light. Print must be large enough for all to read without strain

- **uncluttered** - don't crowd the picture with a confusing welter of facts and figures

fig 3.2

ACTION POINT 17

What advantages and disadvantages can you think of for using flipcharts?

Jot down your answers and then compare them with ours below.

The **advantages** of flipcharts are

- you can prepare simple messages or figures beforehand and reveal them at the appropriate moment

- they will hold a large quantity of data that can be left on display throughout your oral commentary without a distracting hum and light

- they are movable and not dusty

The **disadvantages** of flipcharts are

- they don't look very professional, however skilfully employed

- they are not visually captivating

- the pens could run out

- they are smaller and more awkward to use than chalk or whiteboards

They have many uses such as

- presenting tables

- showing an outline summary of your presentation to help the audience follow your theme. This can be very useful when they are trying to assimilate new concepts such as statistical data

- allowing you to show how statistics were derived in a training session, or recording audience response to information, ie. they are interactive

Overhead Projectors

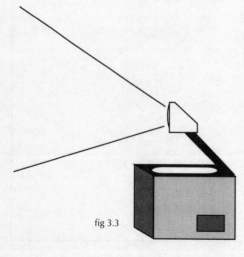

Most of us preparing for a business presentation will be attracted to the overhead projector (OHP) for presenting our ideas and information - and rightly so. It is probably the most visual medium for public speaking, yet it is unsophisticated and easy to use.

If used properly it

- looks professional

- projects a clear visual image of words and pictures

- encourages type-faced words, neat illustrations and a logical flow of thought

fig 3.3

- is mobile, tidy and has few parts to go wrong

■ allows you to return to previous slides

■ is easy to set up

It is a good choice of visual aid for your presentation because

■ the transparencies are easy to prepare

■ you can read what you have written on the acetate without turning away from your audience

■ you can achieve a professional appearance for your work cheaply and without special expertise

■ you can add extra numbers or lines during the course of your presentation to build up a more complex picture without confusing your audience. This means you can save any dramatic figures to add 'live' - this year's improvement in market share, for instance - so long as **you are sure you know exactly what to write and where to write it** during your speech

If you have time, and can plan in advance, you may be able to get professional assistance with preparation. If you will be giving the same talk several times, it is certainly worthwhile to have expert help if it is available - but only **you** know what message you want to convey - your guidance is essential.

One final point - **don't** overload the acetate, it must be legible at the back of the hall. Write in strong, clear colours and do not do more than six or seven lines of **bold** text or numbers on each transparency. Confine yourself to one simple message per projection.

Preparing and Using Transparencies

You will need the following equipment to prepare your transparencies

acetate sheets	cardboard mounting frames
permanent pens	masking tape
scissors	a lettering system
blue crayon	thermocopier or ordinary
photocopier	
graph paper	ruler

If you are preparing your own transparencies, an easy way would be to photocopy a page from a book or report - **don't** - this has little to recommend it, even if you do manage to avoid copyright problems. Photocopied printed text will be illegible to those beyond the second row, the quality will be poor and the information crowded. It's much better to do your own lettering and layout.

So let's look at some guidelines.

Design

You must take into account

■ the variety of purposes for which each type of chart or table is appropriate

■ the nature of the information to be conveyed

■ your audience

In many cases the kind of statistical relationships or quantities you are presenting will suggest a particular chart or table format to use to best bring out their significance. Where these leave scope to choose a format from several types, select the one that will be

■ most appealing to your audience

■ easiest to make attractive on your visual aid

■ best fitted to the overall visual theme you have chosen for the rest of your presentation

Colour and Shading

Use colour and shading constructively to help the audience understand the chart - and your message.

Highlight key areas with the most emphatic colour, or shade them with the most intense shading, such as

■ the first segment of a pie chart

■ the most direct route on a map

When shading, don't use too may lines going in different directions, they confuse the image and have a painful visual impact.

Remember

■ identify which sections are to be highlighted before you begin construction

■ don't advance in the production process without checking samples of your chosen shading to make sure they are visually pleasing

■ use common sense colour keys: green for 'no problem' areas, orange for warnings of potential problems, black for positive quantities, red for negative ones etc

- beware of making contrasts so sharp that the coherence of the image is lost - the whole must 'hang together' even though defining the parts is important

- don't use such dark colours that print will be difficult to read

- don't use the same colour for different things in the chart, eg. the same colour for the title and part of a diagram. It will create wrong associations in the mind of the viewer

Lettering

Prepare the image on an A4 sheet of paper which can then be copied onto an acetate sheet using a thermocopier or an ordinary photocopier. Wherever possible use typeface (not hand writing) and straight, ruled lines.

Lettering can be done by Letraset (transferable lettering on plastic sheets available from graphic art shops) or using a Kroy machine. This works by transferring the lettering you want onto tape strips. Then you simply peel off the backing and arrange them to your satisfaction.

You could do the lettering yourself, but it won't look as professional. Kroy machines are rather expensive but there may be one within your organisation that you could borrow.

To ensure everyone in the room can see the image, use the following size guidelines

Distance from OHP	Size of Lettering
Up to 10 metres	4 mm
10 - 15 metres	5 mm
15 - 20 metres	9 mm

If you do wish to use your own lettering, keep the rows level and the columns straight. Placing a piece of graph paper underneath helps, and if you use faint blue guidelines they won't be picked up by the copier.

If you have access to a computer and laser printer it is very easy to produce high quality lettering which can be printed directly or photocopied onto acetates.

Layout of Transparencies

Try to keep the layout of your transparencies consistent and keep the information on each to a minimum. You don't want to move the transparency once the image is on the screen, so don't use the edges, particularly the top and bottom ones. Keep things simple.

Mounting your Transparencies

Cardboard mounting frames are inexpensive and they help you to store your transparencies. They are essential if you wish to use overlays or 'windows'. They feel quite flimsy before you fix the acetate sheets onto them, but once this is done they become rigid and robust and transport easily. Take care when fixing the acetate sheets to the mounting frames as there is only a small overlap on each side, but masking tape will attach them quite securely.

Building up the Picture

Create anticipation and encourage understanding in your audience by gradually building up the diagram, chart etc.

You can do this in the following ways

■ by using a succession of acetates that gradually make up a total 'picture'. This requires skill to get each of the acetates properly lined up

■ by attaching overlays to the original chart. These when laid on top of the original will line up exactly and add a new dimension by

(i) superimposing new points, eg. continuation of the trend in a line graph

(ii) adding an extra row of figures to a table or matrix - next year's estimates, perhaps

(iii) putting summary or story captions onto the picture to reinforce your commentary - a resumé of the main reasons for significant changes, or a statement of what the changes are - keep it short and simple

■ by using one acetate with a set of coverable 'windows' which can be opened one by one to achieve the same gradual effect

Suppose you want to present the pros and cons of a new customer information area, for example

modern	featureless
comfortable	too crowded
pale colours	soon look shabby

The best way to present these views would be to reveal them one by one. This is achieved by using window masks. These allow you to show blocks of information separately from each other. These are made as follows

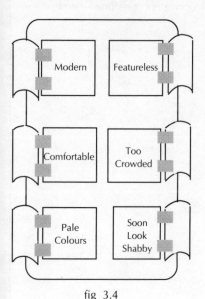

1 Mark on a sheet of paper or card the position of the items on the OHP transparency and cut out the required windows.

2 Replace the windows with card and fasten one of the sides with tape to make a hinge.

3 Make a note on each window of what lies beneath, so you won't show them in the wrong sequence.

fig 3.4

You now want to show the main features of the new customer information area. The best way to present the layout would be to start with the empty area and gradually build up the picture by adding each new feature as you describe it. This is done by attaching overlays to the original transparency, as shown in figure 3.5.

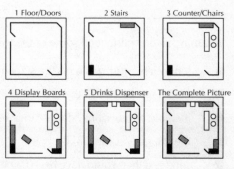

fig 3.5

Let's consider some common mistakes in using the OHP and how we can avoid them.

ACTION POINT 18

Try to recall occasions when you used an OHP or were a member of an audience when one was used. How many unhelpful, distracting or unprofessional events occurred in relation to the OHP?

Make a note of them below then compare them with ours.

You may have experienced some of the following

- too much information on the screen at once

- the image did not fit the screen

- illegible handwriting, double images, old or faulty transparencies

- the image was too small

- solid text that would have been far easier to read from a handout or listen to from the speaker

- the projector was on when it need not have been - it merely distracted your attention

- transparencies were out of sequence

- too much detail that you needed to write down - you had too little time, you could not listen to the speaker at the same time, you could not see your pen and paper in the dark

Let's look at the more important mistakes

(i)   Baffling your Audience

It is possible to fit an enormous amount of material on one transparency. **But do not do what is possible - do what is purposeful**.

(ii)   Cramming and Dictating

Do not use an OHP to cram in columns of text in the expectation that it will be read or even copied by your audience. This is a misunderstanding of what a visual aid should be used to achieve.

If you have a mass of important words - read them, illustrate them, highlight important points visually and provide handouts.

Do not project onto the screen more than the odd few words that need to be copied. Never do this **and** talk at the same time. Simultaneous verbal and visual communications are both distracting and meaningless to your audience. Remember that people can only concentrate on one thing at a time and will not copy accurately if they have to listen and squint while they do so.

Use the OHP to **build up** the important points and **illustrate** them graphically. Do not use it simply as a fancy way of dictating notes.

(iii)   Illegible Images

It is a shame to waste such a useful way of professional communication by projecting - and thus exaggerating and highlighting - amateurish and illegible script and pictorial images. What is acceptable on a chalkboard or flipchart will not necessarily suffice on an OHP.

(iv)   Keystone Effect

This is an optical effect when the beam of light from the projector falling on the screen is not at right angles to the screen. Its effect is to distort the picture on the screen so that in some cases lettering is illegible. The cure is to use the tilt facility found on most screens. Tilt the top of the screen downwards to keep the projected image and screen at right angles to each other.

Photographic Slides

Slide presentations are an excellent way of conveying information, but they are expensive to produce. If the means are available, however, by all means utilise this medium. Remember that people cannot write in the dark, so put the lights on if you are making an important point.

The use of slides is an excellent way of introducing your audience to a piece of new equipment, for example, because you can show on the screen details that it would be almost impossible to show through any other visual medium.

In general, photographic slides are recommended when

■ you can afford the time and money

■ you need a prestigious presentation

■ you wish to create anticipation and expectancy by darkening the room

■ close contact with the audience is not essential

Using sophisticated cameras has become easy during the last two years. Many single lens reflex (SLR) models have automatic focusing built in. Cameras with built in zoom lenses are now available, allowing you to take telephoto, wide angle and close-up shots with the same lens.

Tape-slide

This is an often overlooked medium due to the popularity and ease of using video. It involves the use of two or more slide projectors projecting onto the same area of screen, synchronised to a tape recorder. The tape plays the audio track and also triggers the slide projectors to show the pictures in the correct sequence. Sophisticated dissolve effects can be achieved.

The system gives very high picture and audio quality and is best used with large audiences. It has to be used in a darkened room and considerable setting up time is involved, using the correct audio leads and aligning the projectors on the projection screen. However, used in these circumstances, it gives great impact and costs considerably less than video to produce.

Tape-slide Projection or Video?

Below we deal with video but first it's worth discussing the relative merits of tape-slide versus video. For many presentations, slides are a much more powerful learning aid than video film because you can focus and hold on particular points you wish to make. Freezing the right image on a video film doesn't hold steady and it is difficult to stop at exactly the right frame.

Tape-slide has its disadvantages as well - for example, the changing of slides tends to be quite noisy and we have already said, it's time consuming to set up. If you transfer it onto video, all you need is a TV and a video recorder. But as always with more sophisticated equipment, you must make careful preparations and use the medium properly if it is to be effective.

Video Presentations

There seems to be a belief that the more sophisticated the technology used in presentations the greater the impact. This is partly true - new technology always has the capacity to amaze and thus get the message home by its association with startling effects - but the wise presenter will always weigh the balances between the message to be put across, the situation in which the message is to be delivered and the cost. Video based presentations fall across these categories. Some are poor at fitting in with the structure of your presentation; some are impossible to use because of lack of facilities - lack of an extension lead is an obvious example; and some are extremely expensive to produce. But all are very good at motivating audiences and adding great impact to your presentation.

There are three kinds of medium you can use

- linear video
- interactive video
- computer presentation

Linear Video

The attractions of using a video are obvious

- it is a well known medium
- people know how to relate to video screens
- they are used to its size

Unfortunately they are also well used to the high quality of presentation they see every night in the comfort of their own homes, and they expect, subconsciously or otherwise, to see the same standards wherever a video programme is shown. Such standards are very time consuming and expensive to produce.

Video has other drawbacks as well. It is a linear medium. That is, it is structured to have a beginning, a middle and an end. Most programmes are designed to be seen in their entirety and are complete in themselves. This makes follow-up questions and comments very hard to achieve. It's even harder to stop the programme in the middle and to reinforce conclusions.

Its great advantage is that people do watch it intently.

Video is very expensive to produce. It is highly unlikely that special programmes will be produced for your presentation - unless it is a big media event to motivate participants - in a new training programme, for example. It is even more unlikely that the programme will exactly fit the structure of your presentation.

Keep notes on programmes you have seen which may be useful to you in the future. If the programme is worth it, structure your presentation around it.

ACTION POINT 19

Compare tape-slide and video and decide which would be the most suitable audio-visual aid to use during a presentation, then continue with the text.

Interactive Video

The drawbacks of video can be enthusiastically and expensively overcome by using Interactive Video. This combination of a personal computer and a laservision disk allows accurate searching and displaying of sequences of moving pictures under the command of the computer.

A typical programme might look like this

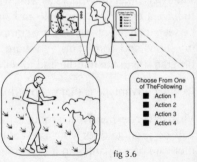

1   The laservision player gives a scenario of a work situation

2   The computer then takes over and asks the user to assess the portrayed situation and choose from a list of answers

fig 3.6

3   The computer then controls the playing of the correct sequence of pictures to show the consequences of the user's choice

The system is capable of great sophistication. You can allow users to

■   assess their own learning style
■   use the program in the way which best suits them

It can also log scores of the user giving good numerical assessment. It is obvious that this system is ideally suited to many training applications but it is unlikely that special Interactive Video programs would be produced for presentations. That, of course, depends on the size and importance of the presentation, but it's worth keeping in mind any training programmes you see which could in part be used in a small presentation. Used in this way, they create an enormous amount of interest in the subject matter you are dealing with.

Computer Presentations

You can use a personal computer to give a very sophisticated presentation at very little cost. You can use the visual display unit (VDU) of the computer like an OHP transparency to

■   list main points
■   display graphs and charts
■   display photographs
■   show illustrations and diagrams

They are usually cheaper and quicker to produce as well. If you are used to spreadsheets and word processing programs then producing well designed charts should be easy for you to do. Store the words and graphics you plan to use in separate, sequentially numbered documents and call them up at the appropriate time.

Recently there have appeared a number of specialist computer programs for use in presentations. They allow you to construct the words of your presentation in an outline word processor, then choose a slide template which includes background shading and text styles and finally automatically merge your words with the slide style. Graphs and charts can be produced and enhanced by a non-specialist to give eye-catching displays. You can print out the displays as handouts. The slide appears at the top of the page and you can add additional notes below its picture.

For output you can

■ send the disk with slide pictures on it to a computer slide bureau who will turn them into 35mm transparencies

■ use the computer itself as the presentation medium

Most programmes allow visual effects such as dissolves between slides to create a very professional effect. You can use the screen itself as the presentation medium. This is useful for presentation to a small group because you can flip backwards and forwards between slides during an informal discussion. Alternatively you can use a liquid crystal display (LCD) platen placed on top of an overhead projector linked to the computer. The LCD platen projects the computer display onto a screen in full colour.

Some computer programs allow the generation of simple animation sequences. They are extremely effective and can be easily controlled by the presenter. A recent development is the ability to record digital video, including sound, to a computer disk from any video source (camcorder, domestic and professional video) and replay it back inside a window in a slide. This is useful for showing short sequences of video for discussion or demonstrations.

The advantages of computer presentations are

■ slides can be rapidly produced and updated

■ sophisticated effects can be produced by non professionals

■ the style of your handouts is the same as your screen graphics, giving a professional look to your work

The system shows all the signs of rapid growth of use. It overcomes many of the problems of video based presentations outlined above, in that it is

■ non linear

■ easily structured to fit in with your presentation

■ capable of being easily restructured for different audiences and presentations

■ professional looking and cheap to produce

The only drawback is the problem of transporting a computer to the presentation venue.

Audio Tape

Do not overlook audio tape as an effective presentation tool. Where words, dialogue or customer relations scenarios are at the centre of your subject matter, the concentrating effect of sound uncluttered by unnecessary images is a very powerful tool.

Its uses may be for

■ illustrating customer relations techniques

■ explaining how to talk on the telephone or use a public address system

■ illustrating noise levels

■ giving examples of customers' opinions

Wherever you want reflective thought from your audience, audio tape can serve you well.

Models, Mock-ups and the Real Thing

If you are presenting a new piece of equipment to an audience, you might consider showing the real thing, and you may be able to pass it around the audience. Touch is particularly effective if you are introducing something like a new fabric for seating.

Displaying models, mock-ups or the object itself eg. a new piece of computer equipment, provides the kind of detail and **'hands-on'** experience unobtainable by any other means.

ACTION POINT 20

Can you think of any disadvantages of passing the real object around the audience?

Jot down any you can think of and then compare them with ours in the text.

There are drawbacks and problems to showing actual objects to the audience

■ passing round objects divides your audience into small chattering groups

■ not everyone can have 'hands-on' experience at the same time

■ you may struggle to be heard or listened to

■ it disrupts the flow of your presentation

Your aim, particularly when demonstrating equipment to the people who are going to have to use it, is to use your presentation to get the **main points across**. These presentations should not be seen as an easy way out of individual tuition or training, which should **follow** your presentation and lead from it.

Unless the object concerned is big enough for everyone to see at the same time, or it is a piece of equipment which the audience members are going to have to use as part of their jobs, you may find that photographic slides (or video) will provide all the advantages of using the actual object or a model, without the disadvantages.

If you do want to use a model, then keep it hidden until the right moment to generate anticipation and avoid distraction from your introductory remarks.

Handouts

Handouts can be very useful to complement your other audio and visual aids. You may be judged on the quality of your handouts as they may well be passed on to other people - make sure they don't let you down. Their usefulness is undeniable **if** prepared and distributed properly.

They could, for example

■ provide the level of detail required by your audience as a pre-requisite for deriving the full benefit of your speech

■ summarise your presentation, leaving your audience free to listen without note-taking

■ recap on detail of particular aspects of your speech such as case studies, examples, surveys or other research

■ show relevant information from instructional manuals

■ suggest further reading or research

■ show individual diagrams or statistical summaries

The important point to remember is to **prepare and distribute your handouts with their purpose firmly in mind**.

If they contain information that needs to be understood **before** you speak, make sure that the members of your audience receive them in good time - that means before they arrive - so that they do not have to read, listen and look at the same time.

Prepare your handouts professionally and thoughtfully - that means neatly-typed, well presented paperwork that uses the same terminology and general language as you do in your presentation This is quite a common mistake - do not use different terminology, quantities or references in your handout notes.

Your handouts may sit in someone's office for months after your words have been forgotten. Make sure they are at least as well prepared and professionally presented as your oral presentation.

Visual Themes

It's valuable to keep **a visual theme** running through the presentation if feasible, whether you only have one or two charts or tables, or a large number of them.

Colour or shading is certainly one factor here, too. Where you are still talking about the same elements of data, but in different contexts, keep the same colours for these elements. For example, if you have a series of charts relating to particular airports, don't change the shadings or colours used to denote those airports for the sake of variety.

The number of different kinds of charts you use can also make the thread of your argument hard to follow, particularly for a general audience. A series of charts each requiring a new explanation of the format for the audience - or at least a sharp mental 'switch' - can cause problems. Yet avoiding boring 'sameness' can be important for some audiences. Again it's a question of **a targeted approach**.

You now have the foundation knowledge necessary to display information visually in a clear context that will allow you to adapt, modify and experiment, but **always err on the side of simplicity**. Try ideas out on paper and discuss them with friends and colleagues first.

ACTION POINT 21

Taking into account all of the media which we have just examined, decide which of them you would use for each of the tasks below

(a)   Demonstrating a new roster system to members of staff.

(b)   Demonstrating a new piece of computer hardware to departmental managers.

(c)   Launching a new training program for all area managers.

(d)   Showing a new design for your department's rest room.

(e)   Discussing ideas for the improvement of efficiency within your section.

(f)   Explaining how to deal with a difficult customer on the telephone.

(g)   Explaining how to deal with a difficult customer face to face (in your work area).

(h)   Discussing how a new piece of legislation affects your department.

(i)   Presenting your departmental performance figures to a small team of managers in a boardroom.

(j)   Getting the company message across, made in a speech by a high ranking executive in the City of London.

Write down your answers and compare them with ours which follow.

There is no wrong answer for any of the situations, provided you adapt the chosen audio-visual aids to fit your presentation. Your suggestions may have been

(a)   A clear set of notes and diagrammatical representation for them to digest and recall when needed.

(b)   The equipment itself - nothing beats first hand, hands-on experience. Handouts with the basic instructions and commands will be useful.

(c)   This is a major training launch and money may be available for a special interactive video program or a slide-tape projection that has been transferred onto video. Whichever medium you choose, it should be professionally prepared and displayed.

(d)   Use an overhead projector with a series of overlays to build up the total picture, slides and possibly handouts.

(e)   An interactive medium would be most suitable, such as a flipchart, chalkboard or whiteboard.

(f)   Audio-tape would be most suitable so that people concentrate on the actual spoken words.

(g)   A visual medium such as video.

(h)   Overhead projector, slides, handouts.

(i)   Handouts, overhead projector, slides.

(j)   You must let the actual words do the work therefore only audio tape with a handout of the text would be suitable.

CHAPTER SUMMARY

Having completed this chapter you should now

■   be aware of the importance of a professional approach to audio-visual aid planning and preparation in order to enhance presentations

■   know the advantages and disadvantages of the various presentation media

■   be better able to make imaginative and intelligent use of the audio-visual aids that are available

■   be aware of the factors to take into account and the techniques to use in order to make well designed and effective charts

If you are unsure of any of these areas, look back and re-read the relevant part(s) of the text.

4 ON THE DAY

So your preparations are complete. You fully understand what is expected of you. Your notes and visual aids are in order and your handouts have been collated and stapled.

In this chapter we shall consider the **last minute preparations** necessary to display and use your audio-visual aids to their best advantage. We shall look at ways of **controlling your nerves** so that you give your presentation to the best of your ability.

4.1 BEFORE YOU GO

Before you set off, draw up a checklist of the things you must remember to take with you. It will include such items as

- the address of the venue, along with a map of how to get there
- the full text of your presentation, note cards and spares
- audio-visual equipment including spare bulbs, screwdriver, masking tape and pens. Take an extension lead - the plug socket may be inconveniently placed
- handouts

Your Appearance

You are in business. You should therefore look businesslike at all times without being flamboyant. However, you are also, for a short time, a performer. Your every feature will be noticed and scrutinised. You therefore need to be **smarter**, **tidier** and more presentable than the average person.

You will not necessarily be judged by your appearance but **how your words sound and are received will be crucially determined by how you present yourself**.

People make instant assumptions from the evidence that confronts their eyes. The same words delivered by the same person in the same way will have a slightly different effect depending on whether the speaker happens to be wearing a dark suit, a pair of jeans or some other form of dress at the time.

You should

- dress comfortably - avoid brand new clothes, tight collars, squeaky shoes, hot heavy jackets etc

- make sure everything you wear is clean, neat and tidy

- not wear anything distracting such as gaudy clothes, heavy perfume or aftershave

- not have anything on you that will encourage a known bad habit

Allow plenty of time to get there, and make sure you know your exact destination. Get directions beforehand - avoid anything that may cause you to panic on the day.

4.2 ON ARRIVAL

Once you have arrived you are going to be very busy. There will be quite a lot of final preparation to be done and there are many things likely to hinder you. Let's look first at your final preparations.

It is very important to provide a pleasant atmosphere in which to give your talk - the audience are more likely to be on your side if they are comfortable. Find the room where you are going to give your presentation and check

1   **The temperature and ventilation** of the room - has the room been shut up for several days with the heating turned up, making it very warm and stuffy? This would make you uncomfortable and your audience restless. On the other hand has some economy conscious person turned the heating off several days ago?

Adjust the heating and windows as necessary so that the room will be pleasant for your audience.

2   **The seating arrangements** - Are there enough chairs to seat everyone comfortably? Should some be removed from the room so that it doesn't look as if only half of your audience turned up?

3   **The lighting** - Are all lights working? Can you dim them? Will one light be sufficient? Will the curtains give adequate blackout for showing your slides? Is the sun shining in and reflecting off the chalkboard?

4   **Noise levels** - Is the room facing a busy main road? Can you close a window to cut out the sound of the traffic?

4.3   SETTING UP THE EQUIPMENT

Once the room and seating are to your liking, you can start setting up the equipment needed to display your audio-visual aids.

1   Test the **television monitor** and **video** - is the tape set at the beginning? Can everyone see it? Make sure the television is switched to the video channel and check the volume and colour. Is the tape set for the start of the presentation? Will everyone be able to see the screen?

2   Clean the **chalkboard** or **whiteboard**. Have you remembered the chalks or pens? Will you need a pointer?

3   Can everyone see the **flipchart**? Have you enough paper? Have you got a spare block? Have you brought enough different coloured pens? Do they write thick enough to be seen from the back of the room? Have you any spares? Is the stand firm and in the best position?

4   Place the **overhead projector** in a position which is convenient for both you and your audience, no more than a step or two from your notes and your collection of transparencies. Arrange the **screen** so that the whole image fills it and does not spill over the edges. Before your presentation begins make sure the image is focused properly and try to avoid the 'keystone' effect by keeping the screen at 90 degrees to the projector.

The transparencies are quite bulky. Put a small table on the other side of the OHP for those you've finished with.

5   Positioning the **slide projector** is often quite difficult to get right, so give yourself plenty of time. If you can use a machine that takes a circular slide tray (Carousel) then do so. It holds up to 120 slides compared with 50 in the straight trays, and it is less likely to stick.

All your visual aids are now ready for the presentation and all that remains to be done is to lay out your OHP transparencies and your note cards on the table, with your full speech beside them. You will not need your speech, but you will gain confidence by knowing it's there. Don't forget a blank sheet of paper for masking the image if you have planned to mask out part of your transparency during your presentation.

Also remember to

■   place the pile of handouts in a suitable corner for giving out at the end of the presentation

■   put a glass of water on the table

Everything is ready for your presentation - you know exactly what you are going to say and your audio-visual equipment is set up.

The final checks should be on your personal appearance. Comb your hair and make sure that buttons and shoelaces are fastened. Check your pockets are not bulging with spare pens or light bulbs for the projector.

There is quite a lot to do for your final preparations and you may have very little time in which to do it, particularly if the room is vacated only a short while beforehand.

And you may be hindered because

■ your hosts are generous in their hospitality

■ some people have come to discuss some business with you and they try to catch you beforehand

■ friends have come to see you and chat about the old days

You will have to be strong-willed, keep an eye on the clock and politely ask their leave to continue your preparations.

The chairperson may want to know something about your past for the introduction. Prepare a note beforehand.

4.4 CONTROLLING YOUR NERVES

If you are not even slightly nervous or keyed up when you have to make a presentation, even to a small group of people that you work with every day, then **you are not doing your job properly**.

Nerves are perfectly normal. Feeling nervous makes the adrenalin flow, it means that your mind and body are functioning properly. They are your body's way of telling you that you are about to do something **special** and that, as a consequence, you are going to have to be at your best or at least at a pitch above your normal approach to conversation.

When under control, nervousness actually improves the quality of what you say and how you say it. It is rare to do consistently worse in 'real' examinations than in 'mock' examinations. The right amount of pressure, fully understood, will bring out the best in you.

So do not try to combat nerves by adopting the attitude that your presentation 'doesn't matter' - you will only make it look that way to your audience.

The most common side effects of being keyed up for a presentation are

- shaking hands and flapping notes
- a dry, squeaky, unreliable voice
- fidgeting
- blanking out and losing your thread (rarer than you might expect)
- getting 'carried away' and saying something you later regret or are embarrassed by

---

ACTION POINT 22

Taking those signs of nervousness which we have just looked at, write down below what you can do to overcome each one.

Check your answers with comments which follow.

You should have written something on the following lines

- keep your hands in a position that does not exaggerate their trembling. Do not hold large pieces of paper. Do not use a long pointer if you are prone to shake

- if your voice lets you down - pause, clear your throat or have a drink of water

- ask a friend what your fidgeting habits are and do what you can to stop them. Do not provide your habits with the raw material they need - loose change, keys, pens to tap etc

- you are not very likely to blank out and loose your thread, but if you do, you have your well prepared notes so that you can soon remedy the problem

- stick to your notes, think before you go off at a tangent, pause before you agree with a comment from the audience

You should remember that

- your nervousness will almost certainly diminish the moment you stand up

- it will be less apparent to your audience than you imagine at the time

- admitting to being nervous will do nothing to improve how you feel or how your audience reacts

Some tips that may help

- try to say something in private just before you stand up so that the first 'squeak' is not made public

- breathe slowly and deeply

- keep your neck and face muscles loose

- have a good look around at the faces of your audience before and just after you start. Do not let **them** do all the staring - try to gain some pleasant eye contact. Smile

- prepare, practise and rehearse in good time

Nervousness is more of a problem before, rather than during, your talk, and there are a number of things you can do to help yourself.

Remember, you do not want to get rid of your nerves altogether because you need the adrenalin, but you can achieve a state of relaxed anticipation.

Throughout life we behave as we are expected to. We adopt different roles at work and in social gatherings. At the start, you could try assuming the role you are expected to play - a confident, professional manager presenting your case. Follow our guidelines closely and very soon you will project this image.

ACTION POINT 23

Make a list of the symptoms of nervousness you think you display when speaking to an audience. Then ask a good friend or close colleague for their opinion.

Put next to each symptom one or more tips for overcoming or lessening that symptom **without adopting an air of casualness**.

Write your comments below and use this checklist as a reminder whenever you next have to make a presentation.

CHAPTER SUMMARY

Having completed this chapter you should now

■   be aware of all the last minute preparations necessary to ensure a professional presentation

■   understand the importance of a professional, appropriate, non-distracting appearance

■   understand the importance of nerves and how to control them

If you are unsure about any of these areas, go back and re-read the relevant part(s) of the text.

5 THE PRESENTATION ITSELF

What you say is more important than how you say it. But if what you have to say is worth saying, then you should not waste the opportunity by saying it badly.

Your poise and body movements, your appearance and the way you use your voice all affect how your audience responds to what you have to say. That being the case you should not leave these matters to chance or take a casual attitude towards them. It makes good business sense to **use** this feature of human psychology to your advantage and take the opportunity to project yourself and your company's values onto a captive audience.

You cannot afford to be a professional, organised and exemplary employee who wastes the opportunity to promote those values in the most public and visible working contexts. In this chapter, therefore, we shall examine **how to make the best use of your voice** to communicate both information and values. We will examine the **effective use of stance and body movements** to project the right image and gain a sympathetic response from your audience. You may well have certain **distracting habits** which we will identify in this chapter so that you can avoid them in the future.

5.1 YOUR POSTURE, PRESENCE AND CONTROL

Although you become a 'performer' before even the smallest audience, you should not be tempted towards flamboyant behaviour in your attempt to be less casual than you are in normal life. A certain amount of professional 'sameness' or 'anonymity' is required in a business context. After all, your aim is to communicate to **all** of your audience, those who would be impressed by waving arms or table-thumping **and** those who would be infuriated by such behaviour.

Develop your own style by all means but stay close to generally accepted codes of professional behaviour which are

Stand and Face your Audience

This applies even if you are talking to a group of your staff at an informal demonstration of some new procedure or equipment, for example.

Let them know

■ **you** are in charge of proceedings now

■ what you look like

■ that you are talking to **them**

If you must turn your back, lean over, bend down or look elsewhere, for example, when writing on the chalkboard, then do not do it while you are talking.

Stand up Straight, Without being Stiff

Look at your audience and hold your note cards at around waist level so that you do not need to drop your head to read them.

Try not to slouch, lean on the table, fidget or make exaggerated hand or arm movements. The adrenalin in your bloodstream will encourage greater than normal movement so try to counteract this by keeping your **arms** as still as you can and letting your **hands** do the work.

If you have ever seen **inexperienced** speakers on a business video tape-recording you will have noticed how wildly they seem to move around.

Nervous Mannerisms

A rehearsal of your presentation with your partner or a close friend may reveal nervous mannerisms you never realised you had.

Do you regularly

■ play with your watch, earring or chain?

■ talk with your hand in front of your mouth?

■ twist your moustache or your hair?

■ push your glasses back on your nose?

These mannerisms are a great distraction as the audience becomes preoccupied waiting for them to happen.

Look at All your Audience

Do not let the audience do all the looking. Use a shallow arc movement of your head - but try not to move your feet unless you have to. Do not shuffle your feet or rock to and fro. Catch an individual's eye for a moment then move on to another. Make sure you look at the ones at the back. Do not let them feel neglected.

Do Not Move and Speak at the Same Time

If you need to move, use visual aids, turn switches or write on a board - keep your speaking during these periods to a minimum without breaking the continuity of your talk. Fit these occasions into natural breaks or links in your presentation - and **put down** pens, pointers, markers and so on as soon as you have finished using them.

Do Not Provide Distractions for Your Audience

Avoid words and phrases such as 'you know', 'and so forth' and 'OK'.

If an extraneous event causes a distraction - a door flies open, a phone starts ringing or a member of your audience has a sneezing fit - then take the initiative to stop it distracting your audience, ask someone to close the door etc.

You are in control. It is your time that is being wasted.

5.2   BODY LANGUAGE

Much has been written on **body language** over the last decade - facial expressions indicate feelings; body posture indicates attitudes and emotional state; gestures emphasise what we are saying.

You should therefore be **aware** of what your physical movements may suggest to your audience and attempt to **use** some of these patterns of behaviour to increase your ability to create the mood you require.

Do not use a tone of voice or facial expression that betrays your words and gives the impression that you think differently. You must be careful to control these when you are communicating with people. Do not forget also that the body language of your audience will tell you whether you are being effective.

Let's look at some examples of body language which you should and should not use

1   **Folded arms** give both a **casual** and a **distant** impression. They tend to suggest that the speaker is confident enough but is not in the frame of mind that wins respect from the audience.

fig 5.2

2 **Straight arms by the side** - you are in effect standing to attention and therefore look smart yet subservient, even frightened. This posture is **never** advisable.

3 **Raised eyebrows** - the automatic way of showing someone near enough to see the effect that you are **friendly**, **welcome** their presence and seek a **response** from them. Try greeting a colleague across the canteen table **without** momentarily raising your eyebrows - it is virtually impossible. In the right circumstances such as a small gathering, this is the perfect way to show you are looking for either agreement, questions or a contribution from the floor. A point, a friendly 'yes' and raised eyebrows will keep the questions and contributions flowing.

4 **Finger and thumb touching** - as if you had a pin between your thumb and index finger. This communicates **exactness.** It is a good way of emphasising the finer points of your presentation. But use it sparingly. Do not devalue its effects before you come to that crucial, fine point. Look at the imaginary pin in your fingers while you hold it and you will create the effect even better.

fig 5.4

fig 5.3

5   **A cutting or chopping movement with your hand** - emphasises something that is imperative. Try this movement in rhythm with the following words

'We **must** reach **our** target **before** June'

fig 5.5

6   **Nodding or shaking your head** - this is explicit and obvious body language and as such should be used **very** sparingly.

If you agree with the contribution of a member of the audience limit yourself to a couple of nods - one to encourage them to continue and another at the end with an accompanying 'yes' or 'I quite agree'. Again use with caution. Too much nodding will be very off putting, especially if you accompany it with the familiar 'yep, yep..' - you will look and sound very strange indeed.

Shaking your head should be used even more sparingly - especially if you are in disagreement rather than sympathy with a member of your audience. It suggests, if used while they are still speaking, that you not only disagree with them but you also want them to stop speaking. It may even provoke a 'No, let me finish'. If you must shake your head only do so **after** the person has spoken.

7   **Face-touching, head-scratching** and **chin-rubbing** should be avoided as they show **insecurity**, **lack of confidence** or a **loss of words**.

8   **Upward eye movements** show you are concentrating on an answer. You are weighing up what has been said, picturing it, assessing it and working out where you stand on the subject. Accompanied by occasional nods and a little tight grimacing it shows you are concentrating and taking seriously the comments you have received.

fig 5.6

Do not do this for more than a couple of seconds, however, or you will lose the attention and eye contact of your audience. If you cannot come up with an instant reply then say so. Do not stare at the ceiling expecting the answer to appear from above.

9   **Clenched fists on the table** indicate your final word on a subject - the issues you are supremely confident of and prepared to defend fiercely. Do not over-use and hence devalue the effect.

You must be aware of the effects of body language and use patterns of physical behaviour intelligently and sparingly.

The time for you to begin your talk has now arrived. The chairperson will introduce you, perhaps by saying a few words about you personally or the subject of your talk.

5.3 YOUR VOICE

You are now on your feet and ready to begin speaking. Let's think about how you are going to deliver your presentation using your voice at the correct pitch and tone whilst speaking clearly and distinctly.

It is a fact of life that even those who are assertive, articulate and clear in normal conversation can be dull, terrified, inaudible, monotonous, hectoring or confusing the minute they stand up in front of both informal and formal audiences.

Nerves are the main culprit - the feeling that all those eyes are focusing on **you** and that they are doing so **together** can unnerve even the most confident of speakers. However, we know that feeling nervous gets the adrenalin flowing which is the body's way of helping us get over our nervousness. You are well rehearsed. You are a confident, professional manager about to give your best for the company.

Your voice is there to be used first and foremost as a vehicle for putting across a controlled, interesting, rational, businesslike message. Remember that most audiences are **not** predisposed to be hostile. You will recall that some, particularly your staff, will want to be **led**, while others will have a stake in your success. The way you use your voice should be based on these facts.

A **misunderstanding** of what is expected of the speaker can often be the cause of bad delivery. Because presentations are **different** and require higher than normal standards, many assume that they should adopt a stiff, pompous or even parliamentary or rhetorical style when they are speaking.

You should be businesslike, adopt an interesting tone of voice, encourage people to like you or at least accept you and let your voice show that you **know** your subject.

It will help if you bear in mind the mnemonic **PAPERS**

Projection
Articulation
Pronunciation
Enunciation
Repetition
Speed

Let's look at each one of these in turn.

Projection

Everyone needs to hear you speak, so your aim is to project your voice to the back of the room without shouting. Your ability to speak loudly without shouting will be enhanced by an upright posture.

You might like to try a little deep breathing before you begin to speak. It can be done quite discreetly. Breathe out to empty your lungs and then breathe in slowly to the count of ten, starting from the bottom of your lungs at the diaphragm and up to the chest. Hold it for as long as is comfortable and breathe out slowly. If you have time, repeat it twice. You will find you have more air in your lungs and your posture will improve naturally, as will your voice projection. An added bonus is that it will help calm your nerves.

In the first few seconds of your presentations check whether everyone can hear you. Asking people at the back of the room if they can hear may establish a rapport with your audience, but it will also spoil your carefully prepared introduction. Instead check by looking at their facial expressions - remember the body language we talked about earlier?

Variety in tone and pitch is very important. If you change the **volume** and **pitch** of your voice - accompanied by a good intake of breath - you will indicate to your audience that you have finished one topic and are about to start another. Listen carefully to TV or radio newsreaders and notice how they introduce a new topic.

If you **raise** your voice slightly you will increase the intensity of feeling that you put into a particular set of words. In general, your aim should be to project your voice to the furthest listener without **ever** shouting. Strange things happen when you shout - your voice changes, your face goes red, your words will not be the ones you intended to say, your audience will be either annoyed, intimidated, embarrassed or deafened.

If you speak a little **more softly**, as though revealing an intimate confidence to your audience, you will increase their collective concentration and encourage them to settle down and be quiet. But keep your softly-spoken parts few and short. Do not tax the patience and hearing of your audience too much - and do not let your sentences, or your address as a whole, tail off by getting quieter as time goes on.

The volume of your voice should also be used for **emphasis**, **effect** and to signal a **break** or **link** in your presentation. Adapt the loudness of your voice to the size of your audience, its **distance** from you and the **acoustic** conditions of the room.

You will probably find that your voice will be higher than usual, so you may wish to make a conscious effort to lower it. If you ever have to give a presentation using a microphone, always try to have a practice session first. There is an art to microphone use and no two microphone systems are the same. Have a rehearsal with a token audience member to give you an assessment of how you sound.

Articulation

Speak distinctly. Do not slur or 'swallow' your words. Do not talk to the floor, the desk, your notes or your chest. Breathing properly will help. Open your mouth and move your lips slightly more than you do in normal conversation. Slightly exaggerate the distinction between words when there may be ambiguity in what you say, for example

> Some others - Some mothers
> Miss de Levine - Mr Levine

If a plural ending in 's' precedes a word beginning with 's' put a tiny break between the two words - pronounce each 's' separately. You may think this happens naturally, but it does not. Unless there is a good reason for having one there is generally no break whatsoever between one word and the next. Listen to someone speaking a language you do not understand. It sounds like one long word.

Emphasise the consonants - the skeleton of a sentence - and the audience will hear you even if your natural voice is on the quiet side.

Pronunciation

We all have certain words which we find difficult to pronounce, and they can ruin an otherwise good presentation. Words like

inestimable

innumerable

statistical

If they cannot be replaced, practice saying them on their own and then in their sentences.

Everyone has an accent so do not worry about yours. In any case you are not going to be able to hide it for more than a few seconds at a time. Indeed accents can be quite attractive and an asset. Regional accents are in vogue these days and certainly more acceptable than they used to be. A little colour and vividness in your voice, so long as you never let slang or regional dialect creep into your presentation, will add to your chances of keeping your audience's attention.

It is far more important to concentrate on pronouncing **difficult** or **commonly mispronounced** words correctly than to worry about whether you say 'pass' to rhyme with 'farce' or 'lass'.

If you are in any doubt how to pronounce a word then check. Dictionaries give phonetic clues to the pronunciation of words, it is normally only a question of knowing where to put the stress.

American pronunciation of many words common in business English is gradually gaining a foothold in Britain. It is for you to choose which you wish to adopt, for example

re**search** (British)   **re**search (American)

Be aware too that many English words are pronounced differently depending on whether they are used as a noun, verb or other part of speech, for example

we conducted a **sur**vey   we sur**veyed** the scene

we accepted the **pro**ject   it was pro**jected** into space

Normally you would not confuse the two - but presentations are not 'normal' occasions.

Finally be aware of **everyone's** liability to utter **malapropisms** from time to time - that is to mistake a word for one that sounds rather similar

'That had always been a bone of contentment (contention) between us'
'Let us confine (confide) a secret'

Enunciation

Emphasise key words, syllables and phrases more than you would in ordinary conversation. Elongate the vowels to add colour and authority to what you have to say

> The standard of customer care is now **waaay** above that of two years ago

Make sure you emphasise the right word in the sentence and, of course, don't overdo the emphasis or you will sound pompous and affected.

ACTION POINT 24

Look at the following sentence, repeated with the emphasis on a different word each time.

Describe the meaning of each and what accusation is being refuted. Write your comments using the space below. Compare them with ours in the text which follows.

(a)   **Busy** executives know that ABC Ltd has greatly improved European services

(b)   Busy **executives** know that ABC Ltd has greatly improved European services

(c)   Busy executives **know** that ABC Ltd has greatly improved European services

(d)   Busy executives know that **ABC** Ltd has greatly improved European services

(e)   Busy executives know that ABC Ltd **has** greatly improved European services

(f)   Busy executives know that ABC Ltd has **greatly** improved European services

(g)   Busy executives know that ABC Ltd has greatly **improved** European services

(h)   Busy executives know that ABC Ltd has greatly improved **European** services

(i)   Busy executives know that ABC Ltd has greatly improved European **services**

Your answer should have highlighted the following points.

(a) Busy executives are aware of the improved European services but perhaps those that are less busy are not

(b) We have got our message across to business executives, if not yet to the non business person

(c) Not only have we improved services but we have got the message across to our customers

(d) ABC Ltd in particular has improved its services

(e) Our customers know, despite anything that's been said to the contrary

(f) Our improvement has been a major one, worthy of note

(g) Far from deteriorating - as some would have you believe - our services have improved and our customers know it

(h) We have done a good job on European services in particular

(i) ABC Ltd offers a good range of convenient European services

Always take the precaution of <u>underlining</u>, **emboldening** or otherwise highlighting the word or syllable to be stressed, for example

> 'We are impressed by a neat appearance, but **un**impressed by poor customer relations'

Repetition

Do not be afraid of repeating yourself, especially if you use a different tone and pitch, not only simple recurring themes and phrases but also **the most important word(s) in your preceding sentence or clause**, for example

> 'The most important person in the eyes of ABC Ltd is the customer, the **customer...**'

Do not let important pieces of information or key issues 'hide' among all the other commonplace words you must utter in your presentation. You should make these words **stand out in high relief**, particularly at the beginning of your address, in order that your audience may grasp at the earliest possible moment what it is you expect them to remember.

A particular politician once said that, if the government ever wished to introduce a 'Slaughter of the Innocents Bill' before Parliament he would be the man to achieve it. He said this without so much as a raised eyebrow from the assembly, so adept was he apparently at camouflaging the momentous among the mundane in his speeches.

Your task is to **communicate** not to obscure - so let your message stand out.

Speed

Very few people speak too slowly in presentations. You are much more likely to speak too hurriedly, either because you cannot wait to get it over with or because you unconsciously adopt the speed you are used to in normal conversation. A good guideline is about 110 words per minute. You can practise this quite easily using either a tape-recorder or a watch while rehearsing.

Try to avoid uttering the ubiquitous 'Er...' or regional variations of it. Better to pause momentarily and start your sentence with a more meaningful word such as 'However...'

Don't forget to pause, it takes a certain amount of courage but is a powerful tool if used well.

> 'Speech is great, but silence is greater'   (Carlisle)

A pause creates anticipation and encourages quiet attention. However, if you are to use the pause effectively, you need to get the length of it right. If it is too long, the audience may think you have lost your place or train of thought.

The pause can be used most effectively

- at the **beginning** of a presentation, both before you greet your audience and immediately after

  Stand.. (pause).. 'Ladies and gentlemen.. (pause).. today I want to..'

- in **mid-sentence**, to emphasise a point or to create anticipation

  'The only way we will end this matter for good... the only way we will put it behind us is to..'

  'I now have the results of that survey and they show conclusively that.. (set up illustration).. the most..'

- **between sentences** to signpost a new theme or change of direction

  '.. we must of course follow normal procedures .. but we could try something new..'

■ at the **end**, for a brief moment at least to show that you are not desperate to finish

You now know exactly what you are going to say and how you are going to say it, so let's look now at how you will use your audio-visual aids.

5.4 USING YOUR AUDIO-VISUAL AIDS

Your carefully prepared audio-visual aids are already in place, it only remains to think about how best to use each one during your talk.

The Chalkboard or Whiteboard

The boards are clean and the chalks and pens are ready. You have reached a point in your presentation when you want to illustrate some important facts.

Remember

■ create anticipation 'and of course the key argument is ..' (write it on the board)

■ use the whole board

■ stop talking whilst you write on the board

■ write clearly and larger than you might think necessary

■ watch your spelling - it is surprising how much more difficult spelling becomes when you are close to the board

■ keep your columns straight

■ clean the board as soon as you've finished with that part of the talk

Don't

■ turn your back to the audience

■ talk to the board as you write

■ press too hard on the chalk - it will break

■ doodle - many a speaker can't resist the temptation to wander back to the board and emphasise the loop on the 'y' or embolden the full stops

■ toss the chalk in the air

■ forget where you last put the chalk down

■ forget to put the tops back on the pens

The Overhead Projector

One of the biggest mistakes is to place the whole transparency before the audience without taking them through it point by point. You should reveal only what you **are talking** about and not what you **are going to talk** about.

If you wish to point things out, it's usually better to do so on the transparency, rather than on the screen. Don't let the image fall on your clothes and face.

Many speakers make the mistake of leaving the OHP on between transparencies. The bright white light is uncomfortable and distracting for the audience. There is also, on some machines, the noise of the fan. **Turn the OHP off** at every opportunity.

Slides

If you wish to discuss a point further and you've finished with the slide on the screen, turn the machine off and put the lights on. Idle eyes will gaze at every detail on the image and ignore what you're saying. It will also enable your audience to see, should they want to make any notes.

Tape-slide Projection and Video

Don't put the television monitor on until you have finished introducing the tape. All eyes will be glued to it rather than to you and all it will be showing is a flickering title or a mass of dots.

Introduce the tape very carefully before you begin. Giving the audience things to look out for and think about while they are watching makes the medium interactive.

Handouts

Distribute any handouts at the end of your talk but tell your audience in advance, especially if they summarise your talk and eliminate note-taking.

CHAPTER SUMMARY

Having completed this chapter you should now

- be better able to use your voice to communicate information and values to your formal and informal audiences

- see the need for a more positive attitude towards the nervousness that accompanies public speaking

- recognise and be able to adopt appropriate stances and body movements to gain and hold your audience's attention and respect

- be aware of the adverse effects of distracting habits

If you are unsure about any of these areas, turn back and re-read the appropriate part(s) of the text.

6 CLOSING THE PRESENTATION

You have given of your best and summarised the main points of your presentation. It is now the turn of your audience to have their say.

In this chapter we look at the types of questions you may be asked and the ways of answering them. You must interpret the type of question you are asked - does the questioner want confirmation that they have understood a crucial factor correctly? Are they offering a different viewpoint? Are they merely talking because they feel they ought to say something? Have they a valid point that you have missed? You must make an instant judgement and act accordingly.

6.1 QUESTION TIME

You may know your talk backwards, but most probably you've crammed a lot of ideas and information into a short space of time. So as you reach the end of your presentation slow down and summarise thoroughly and clearly, iterating the main theme.

Finish on a forceful note, remaining warm and friendly. Smile and invite questions.

When you are asked questions about your presentation, hear each one carefully. In answering all the questions you should be honest, sincere, direct and helpful. If you are, question time will be a satisfying and rewarding experience, and you will sit down to applause.

It is all too easy to take a negative view of question time and be defensive towards your questioners, because you mistakenly believe they

■   are trying to catch you out

■   want to show how much they know

■   feel they have to say something

But in practice, this session fulfils a more positive role

■   you can gauge the feelings of the audience towards your address

■   points of detail can be clarified

■   certain areas of your presentation can be developed

For these reasons you should welcome question time rather than dread it. Look upon difficult questions as a challenge.

In most business presentations people have questions ready, and the chairperson will exercise their privilege to ask the first question. If all then goes silent, don't panic, your audience may be composing their questions or waiting for someone else to ask a question first. Overcome the situation by developing a point you made earlier in a more chatty style.

Usually questions will flow from the start and most will be honest and straightforward. Remember to

- be honest in your answers. If you don't know the answer, say so. Say you will endeavour to find out and let the questioner know

- do not belittle the questioner even if it is obvious to you that the point of your presentation has been completely missed

- repeat and perhaps clarify the question for the rest of the audience - not everyone may have heard the question

- answer statistical questions with words, not more numbers

6.2 DEVIOUS QUESTIONS

You may be asked the odd devious question. But you will be glad to hear that maliciously devious questions are very rare indeed, and in almost all of your presentations the audience will be on your side.

But how do you deal with devious questions when they arise?

- repeat the question for the audience and by doing so change the context

- don't answer the question directly, say something like

  'Let me just clear up one thing first ..'

  Politicians are excellent at dealing with awkward questions without us realising they haven't answered the question that was asked

- show sympathy with the speaker. For example, say

  'I share your concern. It's bothered me for a long time. What I would like to see happen ...'

  then develop the question along lines of interest to you and your audience

Your audience may not have agreed with what you had to say, so listen to the complaints, criticisms or general disquiet of your audience patiently, calmly and professionally.

Yet at the same time you must remain loyal and assertive of your interests and arguments. Listen and understand **but do not concede the logic of your audience's case**. It may be attractive, or even watertight, but the very act of conceding it will encourage them to be more aggressive and even show them the way ahead.

There is a world of difference between for example

and

Do not, under any circumstances, explicitly say or give the impression that you will take back what the audience says to your superiors. Do not become their messenger. If they have used powerful arguments that your superiors or the people you are representing may not be aware of, by all means go back and inform them, but **do not let your audience know** that you will do so. After all, your superiors or whoever you represent should already **know** your audience's views before you are asked to stand before them. If they **do not know,** then admitting the fact will only make your situation worse.

> Remember - **don't react, but respond**

6.3 AFTER THE PRESENTATION

When you've finished your presentation you'll be elated and relieved, but you still have things to do.

You have got to pack up, often in a hurry, so make sure you leave nothing behind - your last transparency on the overhead projector, for instance.

Very often, people will want to talk to you afterwards, and you may wish to have a word with someone in the audience. So beware of the individual who wants to buttonhole you with a question that they were afraid to raise during question time. Politely but firmly get to the people who matter, because invariably there will be a shortage of time after your presentation.

CHAPTER SUMMARY

Having completed this chapter you should now

■ understand the types of questions you may be asked and the ways of answering them

■ know how to deal with awkward or devious questions

If you are uncertain about any of these areas, look back and re-read the relevant part(s) of the text.

REFERENCE LIST

Fast J: Body Language
Pan, 1971

Goodworth C T: Effective Speaking and Presentation for the Company Executive
Century Hutchinson, 1986

Little P: Communicating at Work
Pitman, 1987

Morris D: Gestures - Their Origin and Distribution
Triad Granada, 1982

Morris D: Man Watching - A Field Guide to Human Behaviour
Triad Panther, 1980

Stanton N: The Business of Communicating - Improving Your Communication Skills
Pan (Breakthrough Business Series), 1986

Whitehead P and G: Statistics for Business Pitman, 1984

APPENDIX

We have described some of the more specialised charts and graphs in this appendix

TYPES OF BAR CHART

There are many permutations upon the basic bar chart. We shall look at several of these in turn, in particular looking at the **characteristics** that distinguish one kind of bar chart from another, what **specific kinds of data** each can show effectively and which aspects of the data relationships the different kinds of bar chart will highlight or bring out most clearly.

Grouped Bar Charts

These are sometimes called multiple bar charts; they show comparisons of quantities of two or more items over time.

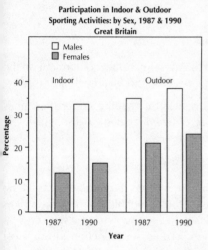

fig 7.1

This chart compares participation by men and women in outdoor and indoor sport in 1987 and 1990.

This chart is undoubtedly effective. Just imagine, for a moment, that the statistics were tabulated and you'll realise how much better the chart shows

- the increase in all sporting activity over the period
- that women's indoor sporting activities have increased more than men's

When drawing grouped bar charts

- distinguish the items being compared by distinctive, clear colours and include a key
- use colours that the audience will associate with the items being compared, eg. summer: yellow, spring: green. Use these colours to simplify your message
- don't include more than three bars in each group of components or the impact will be lost

Grouped bar charts are useful for **comparing information**, such as

■ comparing the number of Domestic, European and Worldwide flights from a particular airport

■ comparing people's characteristics - such as abilities, careers - broken down by age groups, gender etc

■ comparing staffing complements needed to complete certain work as processes evolve or new equipment is introduced

Component Bar Charts

In a component bar chart each bar is subdivided into the different components that make up the whole.

It is usual to

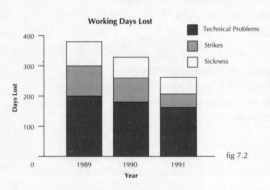

fig 7.2

■ put the most important component on the base line, because this is judged most readily

■ use density of shading rather than lines drawn at different angles to distinguish the components

■ include a key

The chart shows that the number of working days lost through technical problems, strikes and sickness has gone down in each successive year. The most dramatic reduction is in days lost through strike action, which have halved since 1986. This type of chart enables an instant comparison between the component parts.

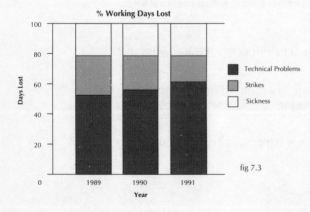

fig 7.3

Percentage Component Bar Charts

In this kind of bar chart, each bar represents 100%. All the bars are therefore the same length, regardless of the total number on which they are based. Each bar is divided up to show the **proportionate share** contributed by **each** of the components, ie. the percentage share of the total for each component.

Because the 100% bar chart has two base lines, one at 0% and one at 100%, it makes the **comparison of components** easier than in the case of the component bar chart. Again do not present a confusing picture by incorporating too many variables. **Keep it simple.**

Look at the chart above. Here the 'working days lost' chart has been drawn as a percentage bar chart. Although the actual numbers of working days lost through sickness have decreased each year (shown in the component bar chart above), they remain exactly the same percentage of the total days lost, ie. 21% each year.

The **percentage** of working days lost through technical problems has **increased** each year, although the **actual number has decreased** each year.

Back to Back Bar Charts

This type of chart can be used in two main situations

■ where you want to present **two sets of data which are related** to each other

■ where you want to display **two distinct categories of data in association**, and a grouped bar chart would be inappropriate because

(i) the scales of the two sets differ or

(ii) the units of measurement differ

Back to back bar charts have two horizontal axes running outwards from either side of the central vertical axis, as shown on the left.

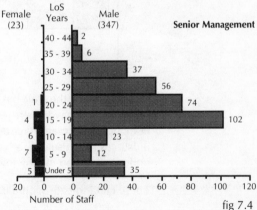

Staff within ABC Ltd by Length of Service (LoS) and Sex at end of March 1992

fig 7.4

Don't forget that, because the units for the scales on the left hand bars can be different from the units of measurement on the right hand bars, you must always make their nature clear to your audience.

Back to back charts can be used for

■ comparing companies' profits, costs, revenues etc over a period of years

■ comparing people's characteristics - such as income or educational qualifications - broken down by age groups, gender or income

Floating Bar Charts

There are two types of floating bar chart

(a)   where the bars extend across the axis of origin

(b)   where the bars are floating entirely within one sector

Where the bars extend across the axis of origin.

Consider the chart below

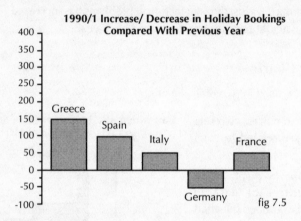

fig 7.5

You can see that the scale has been drawn so that there is a zero line below which minus values have been recorded. This shows that the number of holiday bookings to Germany have decreased when compared to the previous year. This illustrates how useful this type of bar chart can be to managers in monitoring performance and identifying areas where improvement may be needed.

These can indicate such data as

■   the number of tasks completed on schedule (in the positive sector of the graph) and the number completed behind time (in the negative sector)

■   the percentage of flights arriving on time and the percentage delayed

■   the number of orders completed within estimated price and the number exceeding it

Where the bars are floating entirely within one sector

Consider the chart below.

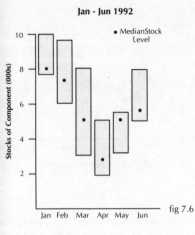

Jan - Jun 1992

fig 7.6

This chart shows the monthly maximum and minimum component stock levels. It is possible to include additional information such as the **average** value. Our example shows the **median** stock level. These supplementary markers must, of course, be interpreted in a key.

Floating bar charts can indicate such data as

■ the highest and lowest prices of a commodity

■ the maximum and minimum sales revenue over a series of days, months or years

■ the maximum and minimum numbers of customers served by different companies

Bar charts are just one form of statistical representation, though very useful and versatile tools if used imaginatively.

LINE CHARTS

In this chapter we shall look at

■ scatter diagrams

■ band charts

Scatter Diagrams

Scatter diagrams are plotted using two axes at right angles in exactly the same way as a line graph. Scales and units of measurement must be included. They are the simplest way of showing whether there is a relationship between two variables.

Consider the two diagrams.

In diagram (a) there is a strong correlation between

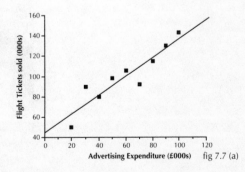

fig 7.7 (a)

the money spent on advertising and the number of ticket sales. An increase in the amount of money spent on advertising results in more flight tickets being sold.

In diagram (b) there is no evidence of correlation. The flight distance appears to have no correlation with delayed arrival time.

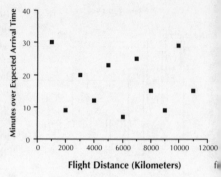

Band Charts

Where you have a number of competing variables changing over time, you can use a band chart. This is a variation of the multiple line graph, in which the areas between the lines are shaded. The band chart below, for example, effectively illustrates the number of passengers carried each year by major airlines operating on the same routes.

The shading draws attention to the differences between the market shares of the three airlines on this route and how they have varied. It directs our attention immediately to questions such as

■ why did Airline A lose so much traffic to Airline C at the beginning of the period?

(A major advertising campaign by Airline C? A price war? Internal problems within Airline A?)

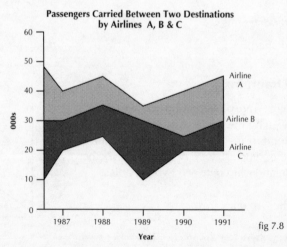

fig 7.8

■ why did Company C suffer so badly during the 1988 - 1989 recession on the route?

But the band chart presents problems

■ it can only work where the various factors being illustrated **never** change their ranked order over time. This means it can only be used when the dominant factor (ie. largest) does not dip below its nearest rival at any point

■ it can only work effectively where the factors being illustrated are **competing**

The band graph then is a useful tool in the right circumstances. It is good for showing competitive positions.

PICTOGRAMS AND MAPS

You might consider a more pictorial representation of your statistics by the use of pictograms or maps.

Pictograms

In pictograms, a symbol is used to represent a unit of measurement. For example, you might draw a row of car-shaped symbols in which each of the symbols represents one hundred cars sold.

The final symbol for the year 1990 would stand for 500 cars. Your audience can see at a glance that the number of car sales has steadily increased each year.

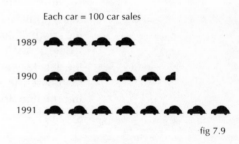

fig 7.9

This is a fashionable technique for livening up statistical presentations especially in television news.

There are however disadvantages

■ unless you have access to professional standard illustrations, your pictograms may look shabby and amateurish

■ they are no good for expressing detail (imagine trying to distinguish between one fifth and one quarter of a car in the above example)

■ they can seem patronising or childish to your audience if used in the wrong circumstances

However, in the right atmosphere such as one that includes an element o publicity or promotion - they can be extremely captivating and look professional

Maps

Any **factors that vary regionally** in a way that is significant to your presentation could be expressed in a map. Consider the map below .

This shows that rain falling on the eastern side of Britain has a lower pH (ie. i more acidic) than rain falling on the western part of Britain.

Maps can also be used in combination with other charts, eg. the number o domestic flights from UK airports could be represented by a series of bar charts at the appropriate location on the map.

These are expressive and interesting ways of illustrating statistics but remember

■ they must look professional

■ they must show the information **first**, entertain second. In many contexts the information would be lost in the detail of the map. Keep the information to the forefront

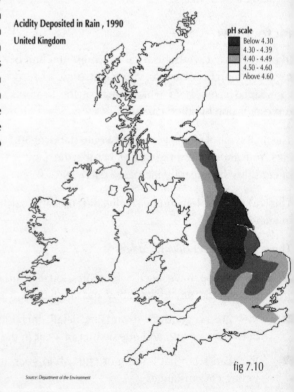

Acidity Deposited in Rain , 1990

United Kingdom

pH scale
Below 4.30
4.30 - 4.39
4.40 - 4.49
4.50 - 4.60
Above 4.60

Source: Department of the Environment

fig 7.10